The Whimsic Alley Book of Spells

BOOKS BY GEORGE BEAHM

Vaughn Bode Index (Heresy Press, 1975)

Kirk's Works: An Index of the Art of Tim Kirk (Heresy Press, 1977)

How to Sell Woodstoves (George Beahm, Publisher, 1980)

How to Buy a Woodstove—and Not Get Burned (George Beahm, Publisher, 1980)

Notes from Elam (as editor/publisher, GB Publishing, 1983)

The Great Taste of Virginia Seafood (as editor/publisher, GB Publishing, 1984)

How to Publish and Sell Your Cookbook: A Guide for Fundraisers (GB Publishing, 1985)

Write to the Top: How to Complain and Get Results—Fast!
(The Donning Company, 1988)

The Stephen King Companion (Andrews McMeel Publishing, 1989)

The Stephen King Story (Andrews McMeel Publishing, 1990)

War of Words: The Censorship Debate (Andrews McMeel Publishing, 1993)

Michael Jordan: A Shooting Star (Andrews McMeel Publishing, 1994)

The Stephen King Companion: Revised & Expanded
(Andrews McMeel Publishing, 1995)

The Unauthorized Anne Rice Companion (Andrews McMeel Publishing, 1995)

Stephen King: America's Best-Loved Boogeyman (Andrews McMeel Publishing, 1998)

Stephen King from A to Z (Andrews McMeel Publishing, 1998)

Stephen King Country (Running Press, 1999)

Stephen King Collectibles (Betts Books, 2000)

The Unofficial Patricia Cornwell Companion (St. Martin's Press, 2002)

Essential J. R. R. Tolkien Sourcebook (New Page Books, 2003)

How to Protect Yourself and Your Family Against Terrorism (Potomac Books, 2003)

*Muggles and Magic: An Unofficial Guide to J. K. Rowling
and the Harry Potter Phenomenon* (Hampton Roads Publishing, 2004)

*Fact, Fiction, and Folklore in Harry Potter's World:
An Unofficial Guide* (Hampton Roads Publishing, 2005)

Passport to Narnia: A Newcomer's Guide (Hampton Roads Publishing, 2005)

Caribbean Pirates: A Treasure Chest of Fact, Fiction, and Folklore
(Hampton Roads Publishing, 2007)

*Muggles and Magic: An Unofficial Guide to J. K. Rowling and the Harry Potter
Phenomenon*, 3rd ed. (revised and expanded, Hampton Roads Publishing, 2007)

Stephen King: American Storyteller (Flights of Imagination, 2007)

Stephen King Collectibles, 2nd ed. (revised and expanded, Betts Books)

Discovering the Golden Compass: A Guide to Philip Pullman's Dark Materials
(Hampton Roads Publishing, 2007)

The Whimsic Alley
BOOK OF SPELLS

Mythical Incantations for Wizards of All Ages

Edited by
George Beahm
and **Stan Goldin**

Illustrations by Tim Kirk

HR
for the evolving human spirit

HAMPTON ROADS
PUBLISHING COMPANY, INC.

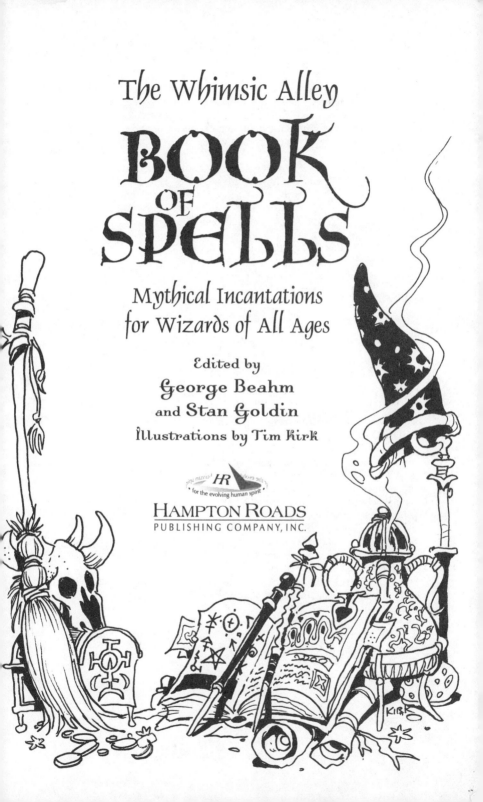

Cover design by Steve Amarillo
Cover and interior art © 2007 by Tim Kirk
Photos © 2007 by Whimsic Alley

Hampton Roads Publishing Company, Inc.
1125 Stoney Ridge Road
Charlottesville, VA 22902

434-296-2772
fax: 434-296-5096
e-mail: hrpc@hrpub.com
www.hrpub.com

If you are unable to order this book from your local
bookseller, you may order directly from the publisher.
Call 1-800-766-8009, toll-free.

Library of Congress Cataloging-in-Publication Data

The Whimsic Alley book of spells : mythical incantations for wizards of all ages /
edited by George Beahm and Stan Goldin.
   v. cm.
   Contents: What you need to know about this book / by George Beahm -- A history of Whimsic Alley ; Magiques and maglinots / by Stan Goldin -- Spells. Love
and emotion spells ; Practical spells ; Time, space, and weather manipulation spells ;
Dueling spells ; Communication spells ; Miscellany spells ; Whimsic Alley spells --
Wizard wears, wares, and where? / by Stan Goldin -- Wizard wear : assembling a
wizarding wardrobe ; Creating a bewitching wardrobe ; Wizard wares : wands ;
Wizard where? A visit to Whimsic Alley -- Extracted chapters from the Whimsic
Alley Book of Knowledge / by Stan Goldin -- Where do wands come from? ;
Mastering a spell ; Spells, charms, hexes, curses, and jinxes.
   Summary: Provides more than 200 spells contributed by Harry Potter fans
worldwide, as well as guidance on selecting an appropriate wardrobe, a history of
wands, and other related topics.
   ISBN 978-1-57174-535-4 (alk. paper)
   [1. Magic--Fiction. 2. Wizards--Fiction. 3. Witches--Fiction. 4. Fantasy.]   I.
Beahm, George W. II. Goldin, Stanley, 1950-
   PZ7.W57654 2007
   [Fic]--dc22
                                2007001823

ISBN-13: 978-1-57174-535-4
ISBN-10: 1-57174-535-1
10 9 8 7 6 5 4 3 2 1
Printed on acid-free paper in Canada

To my son Reid, whose childhood desires spawned my own second childhood. Had it not been for him, I might still be balancing ledgers rather than casting spells. My own dreams are materializing, in large part, because of his willingness to sleep on a couch for two years—how he must have yearned, in those days, for even a closet beneath the stairs that he could have called his own.

And to Sue, who has always been there for me—helping me endure my burdens, sharing my successes, providing the aforesaid couch, and being my best friend in every way possible. I have to admit that I have fallen hopelessly under her spell.

—STAN GOLDIN

The fantasy writer's job is to conduct the willing reader from mundanity to magic. This is a feat of which only a superior imagination is capable, and Rowling possesses such equipment. She has said repeatedly that the Potter novels are not consciously aimed at any particular audience or age.

—STEPHEN KING, in a review of *Harry Potter and the Goblet of Fire,* published in the *New York Times* (July 23, 2000)

Table of Contents

— INTRODUCTION —

What You Need to Know about This Book

BY GEORGE BEAHM

t a book signing in the spring of 2006 at Whimsic Alley, in the company of artists Tim Kirk and Britton McDaniel, I was approached by Stan Goldin (the proprietor of Whimsic Alley) with an interesting proposition: Would I be interested in editing a book of spells?

I told him I would be.

As it turned out, Stan had been asked—pestered, in fact—by younger customers for a spellbook, since most of the existing books were for practicing Wiccans. By default, Stan carried a selection of Wiccan texts, but they lacked the fun, the whimsy, of imaginary spells.

Stan's inspired idea was to hold a contest in which prizes would be awarded to the best submissions. Of course, not everyone can be a winner, but to have a spell published herein is a rewarding experience in itself.

From the young to the young at heart, then, the spells came in from all over the world. The youngest spell caster is a delightful nine-year-old girl named Claire, who lives in Williamsburg, Virginia, as do I. The oldest is Whimsic Alley founder Stan Goldin, with me (alas) nipping at his heels.

Stan sorted the spells out by subject matter and made the initial cut, sending 300 of the best to me. I then made the final cut, down to approximately half that. Since the prizes were drawn from Stan's store, he had the joy of selecting the prize-winning spells.

The result, we hope, is a whimsical book that will make you smile, laugh, grin, or nod your head knowing that a certain spell is just what the witch doctor ordered.

Here's hoping this book casts a spell on you, just as its contributors cast a spell on both Stan Goldin and me, without the need to cast the Appreciation Charm (look it up in this book).

And a personal note of thanks to Stan: Thanks for letting me hob-nob with a fellow wizard such as yourself on this thoroughly whimsical project!

Stephen King, in one of his many nonfiction pieces, told about a letter he had gotten in the mail from a young boy who, King said, resembled a character out of a Gary Larson cartoon. The boy had sent him two photos: one photo was of him labeled "me" and the other "me with a monster." The photos were identical. In one photo, the boy *imagined* himself with a monstrous creature on his arm.

I kept that image in mind as I reviewed the spells submitted for this book because the submissions were all about engaging one's imagination, about seeing not only what's in front of our eyes but also seeing what's *not* there. Again: the power of imagination.

In editing the spells, we decided to avoid the awkwardness of being gender specific and using "s/he" or inelegant variations thereof. In this book, "he" refers to either "he" or "she." Similarly, "wizard" is a reference to both witches and wizards, which is consistent with current usage not only among nonmagical people, but also among the wizarding community at large.

Most of the spell incantations are written in Latin, which is the favored language for spell casters worldwide. A universal language, it allows a wizard to communicate with fellow wizards without fear of mistranslation.

Finally, in selecting the spells for inclusion in this book, we rejected many fine submissions. Many extremely creative spells went beyond the boundaries of what we felt an ordinary wizard should be capable of doing. Therefore, spells which changed the rotation of the Earth or which, with the flick of a wrist, ended global warming, were rejected as implausible. Some submitted spells were humorous, but we couldn't figure out why anyone would ever want to employ them. Many of the spells we received were very similar to each other. In such cases, where all things were fairly equal, we may have given greater weight to younger contributors or to submitters who were not represented elsewhere in the book. In other cases, we flipped a coin. Each of you who feels your spell was unfairly rejected should feel free to cast your curse on us, the editors, for exhibiting our all-too-human failings.

A History of Whimsic Alley

BY STAN GOLDIN

himsic Alley has its roots in an ancient legend of a magical marketplace that randomly appears and disappears. The earliest tales date back nearly three thousand years ago. Purported visitors over the centuries have told such outlandish tales about Whimsic Alley that they were typically branded as lunatics or heretics. (It's a little-known fact that the word "whimsy" was derived from tales of Whimsic Alley. Any outrageous tale became a "flight of whimsy" and its tellers were speaking "whimsically.") Sadly, of the thousands of purported visitors to Whimsic Alley, most were either executed or banished to asylums. It's suspected that many potentially credible sources were therefore reluctant to come forward. The legend, it's said, was documented in a series of volumes entitled *Tales of Whimsic Alley,* but all known copies were destroyed in a series of witch hunts.

In 1354, Sir Geoffrey Whilsey, a renowned wizard with the gift of clairvoyance, proclaimed he had visited the legendary Whimsic Alley. The experience, he said, profoundly changed his life. Because of his stature, Sir Geoffrey was not ostracized, but he was widely ridiculed nonetheless. Thereafter, he never had much credibility.

Sir Geoffrey changed his name from Whilsey to Whimsic and began boasting that he would one day build his own Whimsic Alley, a marketplace like no other—the first to cater exclusively to the magic community. To keep outsiders away, he would cast a cloaking charm on the marketplace, making it invisible to nonwizards. Then, so that wizards the world over could experience his vision, he would make Whimsic Alley nomadic. The entire marketplace would move to a new location every several years.

People took everything he said with a grain of salt. However, in 1367, some twenty years after he first proclaimed visiting the mythical marketplace, Sir Geoffrey's dream became a reality. Whimsic Alley opened in Dublin to great fanfare.

The early years were difficult. People seemed reluctant to go to a place called Whimsic Alley, since the myth of such a place had such dubious notoriety. Making matters worse, Sir Geoffrey practiced a rather rare form of magic, so his cloaking charm had inadvertently hidden the Alley from nearly everyone.

Approaching bankruptcy, Sir Geoffrey took on a partner—the renowned French cloak maker Rene Habber. With the addition of Habber's Cloak Shop, Whimsic Alley began drawing customers. Its newfound credibility attracted other merchants as well.

Sir Geoffrey relinquished control of the marketplace to Habber. He was forced to take a back seat to this rag merchant, some twenty years his junior. Though the partnership worked well financially, Sir Geoffrey and Habber came to despise each other.

In 1389, Habber moved the nomadic marketplace from Dublin to Paris, where it prospered. Rather than celebrating his now burgeoning business, Sir Geoffrey seemed to resent Habber's success at the helm. He was being pushed further and further into the background. He began drinking heavily, and entered into an affair with Habber's wife. When Habber learned of the affair, he challenged Sir Geoffrey to a duel in which he cast a transformation spell on Sir Geoffrey, turning him into a tree sloth. The spell, regrettably, proved irreversible and Sir Geoffrey, founder of Whimsic Alley, lived his remaining days hanging from the branch of a large sycamore tree.

As an intentional affront to Sir Geoffrey, Habber changed the name of Whimsic Alley to Rue Habber and positioned a street sign with the name directly opposite the tree that Sir Geoffrey then called home. The marketplace remained Rue Habber for eighty years until Habber's grandson, Frederick Dasher, changed it back to Whimsic Alley in tribute to Sir Geoffrey, whom Dasher learned was his true biological grandfather.

Frederick's son, Stanley Dasher, had a roommate at the Alsone Wizarding Academy in Brussels named Reid Axelrood, whose family owned Phoenix Wands, the world's preeminent wandmaker for nearly two millennia. The Axelrood family also owned the bleeding forest, from which the world's finest wands are made. Reid promised his best friend, Stanley, that he would someday relocate the family business to Whimsic Alley. The opportunity came just two years later. Reid inherited the business when his father and uncle died in a freak accident and moved it to his friend's marketplace as promised. With Phoenix Wands there, Whimsic Alley had finally arrived. It was now *the* place for the magic community to shop.

Other prominent businesses eventually relocated to Whimsic

Alley. Sue Pilcher's gourmet wizard confections merged with Roberta Bott's. Widdleshaft's Quill Shop moved there in 1780 and Danielle Esterhaven's Curio Shop sprung up in the late nineteenth century.

Over the centuries, the nomadic marketplace has been in 112 locations around the world. In 2004, with the swish of a wand, Whimsic Alley moved to its first American location in Santa Monica, California, its current location.

Whimsic Alley
2717 ½ Wilshire Blvd.
Santa Monica, CA 90403
Phone: 310-453-2370
Fax: 310-453-2374
Website: www.whimsicalley.com
Email: CustomerService@WhimsicAlley.com

Magiques and Maglinots

BY STAN GOLDIN

hose of us capable of performing real magic, not merely illusion and deception as performed by popular entertainers, live in a world called Magique. It is parallel to and complementary with the nonmagical world. Its inhabitants—witches, wizards, sorcerers, goblins, elves, leprechauns, seers, sages, conjurers, and magical creatures of all kinds—are collectively referred to as Magiques. They are called that to distinguish themselves from noninhabitants, who are called Maglinots (a colloquial offshoot of this term is Maggles, with other spellings common throughout the world).

The Maglinots falsely believe that the evolutionary spiral stopped with them, as though they are on the surface of the giant genetic stew and all future developments shall occur beneath the surface. As we know, the Magique is an advanced state that we have evolved into.

As a natural part of the evolutionary cycle, many new Magiques, born of Maglinot parents, come along every day. Many within the Magique community, particularly those with long bloodlines and rich heritages, consider themselves superior to Nouveau-Magiques, and refuse to associate with them. However, many Nouveau-Magiques, with proper training, are every bit as adept at magic as are their purebred counterparts. Chances are, if you felt compelled to pick up this book, you have sensed that you belong among the Magiques, even if you were born of Maglinot parents.

As a convention in this book, when we refer to Magiques, we are referring to inhabitants of the magical community. When we refer to Maglinots, we are referring to noninhabitants of the magical community.

SPELLS

Most of the spells are invented, but some of them have a basis in what people used to believe worked. We owe a lot of our scientific knowledge to alchemists!

—J. K. Rowling, in an interview for Amazon.com

Love and Emotion
SPELLS

A Love Charm
by Amanda Schmer

— SPELL INCANTATION —
"Affection complexious"

— DESCRIPTION —
This spell causes the receptor of the charm to fall in love with the spell caster. The spell will be gradual in its effect, so it is not easily detected. Only the spell caster can lift the charm.

— SPELL —
Think of love and passion while flicking your wand up and to the right diagonally, and then back down and to the left diagonally.

— COUNTERSPELL —
"Insufferable simplexious"

A Spell to Converse with Deceased Loved Ones

by Mulva B.

— SPELL INCANTATION —

As the crackle of the candle proceeds and persists,
remembrance of loved ones who are surely missed.
For one last conversation, crumpets, and tea,
bring the one that has gone from me.

— DESCRIPTION —

This spell is used to talk with a deceased loved one.

— SPELL —

Flick your wand twice over a lighted candle and say the incantation.

— COUNTERSPELL —

As our time together melts like the candle,
I put this picture back on the mantle.
The crumbs that remain and the tea leaves so soggy,
my memories now are much less foggy.
Return [cite name here] to where he belongs,
our time together was so short—yet long.

✶ Wizard Persona ✶

Mulva recently opened a local chapter of the National Sarcasm Society in Indiana, Pennsylvania, where she is currently attending college. She is an Heiress of Thrown Sarcasm, a title she's held for five years.

A Spell to Make Amends
by Ivy

— SPELL INCANTATION —
"Colligo amica clementius"

— DESCRIPTION —
This spell stops two friends from fighting by making them suddenly forget why they were having a disagreement.

— SPELL —
The spell caster must be a mutual friend of the two friends who are having a disagreement. The spell caster must think of a time when the three of them were laughing together and then say the incantation, "Colligo amica clementius."

✶ Wizard Persona ✶

Ivy is a healer and can transform into an owl to fly to witches and wizards in need.

A Spell to Remove the Fear of Exams

by Magnolius

— SPELL INCANTATION —

"Remove my fear of exams!"

— DESCRIPTION —

This spell takes away the fear of exams from whoever is put under it. It might be used for midterms or end-of-year exams.

— SPELL —

Think only of the subject to be tested on and say, "Remove my fear of exams!"

✶ Wizard Persona ✶

Magnolius is in charge of a cat-sitting service for witches and wizards.

A Spell to Repair a Broken Heart

by Ivy

— SPELL INCANTATION —

"Liber cardiacamo"

— DESCRIPTION —

This spell frees someone from pining over an unrequited love.

— SPELL —

Caster should trace a heart in the air and say, "Liber cardiacamo."
(This spell can be cast on oneself or someone else.)

⋆ Wizard Persona ⋆

Ivy is a healer and can transform herself into an owl and fly to witches and wizards in need.

The Healing Heart Spell

by Crystalia

— SPELL INCANTATION —
"Healiano hearticus"

— DESCRIPTION —

When a heart is broken, this spell helps lift that person out of his depression. Although it doesn't take away all the pain, it helps build up an ability to help overcome the crushing feeling associated with being heartbroken.

— SPELL —

Say the spell, "Healiano hearticus."

— COUNTERSPELL —
"Evilunatus heartica"

★ Wizard Persona ★

Crystalia is the brave, older sister of Michaela the Quick. Known for her magical touch with children and animals alike, Crystalia is even tempered and quick witted. She enjoys reading, as well as writing, a good story.

The Memory Eraser Spell
by Olivia Wenshoft

— SPELL INCANTATION —
"Forgiquellom"

— DESCRIPTION —

This spell erases the memory of any particular event that embarrassed you, in any person you choose. You must have been a victim of the event; for example, you tell your best friend (or so you thought) that you like a boy, and that friend tells the boy right in front of you. You can erase this memory/information from the boy, your ex-friend, and anyone else standing there at the time.

— SPELL —

Grit your teeth, take a deep breath, close your eyes, and say to yourself the names of all the people present at the event. Then open your eyes, sweep your wand from left to right in one long motion, and say the spell, "Forgiquellom."

— COUNTERSPELL —

In the event you erase the memory of the wrong person (for example, someone with the same name who is standing a few feet from the intended person), you must stand in front of that person, flick your wand twice, and say, "Ker-choo" and the person's name. His memory will then be restored.

✳ Wizard Persona ✳

Olivia Wenshoft comes from a long line of servants who serve the Duchess of Torshaven. The Wenshoft family has served the Royal Family of Torshaven since 1706. She is the first in her family to attend a school of magic.

The Mother's Arm Charm

by Professor Miranda Tealeaves

— SPELL INCANTATION —
"Somnus"

— DESCRIPTION —

This charm can be used on a young child, or anyone under extreme duress. The spell wraps an invisible arm of comfort around the person, allowing his head to nestle against an invisible shoulder. The person will feel as though he's being gently rocked as he falls asleep listening to the comforting sound of a heartbeat.

— SPELL —

1. Lay the person down.
2. Tap the person on the head with your wand and say, "somnus."
3. Make one quick, counterclockwise circle with the wand to the source of anguish.
4. Make two clockwise circles (one for the comforting arm, and the other to start the heartbeat) and tap the person on the forehead.

— NUANCES —

In order for the charm to be successful, the spell caster must stay with the person until he is asleep.

✳ Wizard Persona ✳

Miranda left France in 1872 for the New World. She is known for creating the Mars Academy, the first formal school of magic in the New World. She currently resides in Lynnwood, Washington, just a short broom ride from campus.

The Music Spell
by Professor Tanner

— SPELL INCANTATION —

"Music amorum singum"

— DESCRIPTION —

This spell makes a person love to sing whenever possible. It also makes the person more cheerful as a result. A person might use this spell if he was very upset, unhappy, or just a bad singer!

— SPELL —

Think of music that you would like to hear. Keep your wand steady when saying the spell. Repeat the spell three times.

— COUNTERSPELL —

"Music hatum singum"

⋆ Wizard Persona ⋆

Professor Tanner is a Professor of Magic and the headmaster's assistant. He is credited with the creation of several important spells. He currently resides in Emmaus, Pennsylvania.

The Peace Spell

by Hera Alexa

— SPELL INCANTATION —
"Sssshhhh-quietet"

— DESCRIPTION —

This spell makes people forget why they're fighting so that they stop. This spell is good for present and future wars.

— SPELL —

1. Think of a peaceful place.
2. Twirl your wand three times, and then draw a peace sign.
3. Speak the spell.

★ Wizard Persona ★

Hera is a witch of Greek descent. Her name was derived from Hera, the wife of Zeus, and Alexa, the defender.

The Protection Spell
by Tonya Brisson

— SPELL INCANTATION —
"I protect thee . . ."

— DESCRIPTION —

This spell protects any person or creature you love.

— SPELL —

1. Find a picture of the person or creature you wish to protect, and place that picture in a clear, lidded, plastic container.
2. Fill the container with happy artifacts, such as rose petals, love letters, etc.
3. Use your writing hand and position it over the container.
4. Using a circular motion with your hand over the container, speak the following: "I protect thee [name of person or creature being protected] with all my heart. May you be healthy and happy for all the days to come. May no dark forces find you. Blessed be."

— COUNTERSPELL —

Empty the container.

✶ Wizard Persona ✶

Tonya is a married mother with two children, Austin and Sydney. She is a nature-loving witch who can talk to animals telepathically.

The Relaxation Spell
Thoughts of Sanctuary
by Sara Kiwa

— SPELL INCANTATION —
"Anges en vol, anges in vol"

— DESCRIPTION —
This spell lets the user come into a state of peace and relaxation. It's best used when under stress. It can also be used when on a vacation. Let the mind take a break and forget that important meeting with the boss or that parent-teacher conference after school so you're not in a worried state of mind.

— SPELL —

1. Clear your head and try to mentally drown out the noise surrounding you.
2. Look to the sky and sing these words in French: "Anges en vol, anges in vol" (translation: Angels in flight).

— COUNTERSPELL —
"Nouvelle terre"

★ Wizard Persona ★

Sara Kiwa grew up in Berlin, on the small Drive of Leuchtkäfer. She is known for her awe-inspiring poetry. She currently is in search of her inner spirit while on retreat in the Himalayan mountains.

The Revolving Emotion Spell

by Hevaluscem

— SPELL INCANTATION —

"Emotis occulto"

— DESCRIPTION —

This is an extreme spell that enables the spell caster to transfer a part of sadness from another person. It can be used when close friends or relatives are deeply depressed, when the psychic pain is obviously unbearable and apparent to the spell caster.

— SPELL —

This spell is not only difficult to perform, but it is also dangerous for the spell caster. In fact, to make this spell function, the spell caster must not be sad because those emotions would be transferred in part to the other person's feelings.

There's also the danger that if you lose too much of your own feelings in the process, you may lose your own emotions and humanity and, as a result, become depressed and angry. It is best to use this spell sparingly.

This is a nonverbal spell. You must have happy feelings in your heart, think of the spell, and give a little flick of your wrist, up and down.

✳ Wizard Persona ✳

Hevaluscem is 21 years old and is greatly interested in animals and magical spells. She is currently studying magic and hopes to have a career in magic in the world of spirit, including helping others realize their dreams or looking after animals. She has a cat named Zéo and a crow named Anubis.

The Spell to Make Your Troubles Temporarily Disappear

by Heather

— SPELL INCANTATION —

"Diluo"

— DESCRIPTION —

This handy spell takes away your troubles for a day so you don't dwell on them. It should only be used for trivial problems.

Caution: Just because you have temporarily forgotten them, it doesn't mean your troubles have disappeared. You still will have to deal with them at some point.

— SPELL —

Focus on your worries, and then place the tip of your wand to your temple and say, "Diluo."

✶ Wizard Persona ✶

Heather, who often uses wandless magic, has been breeding phoenixes at her home since 2000.

The True Love Spell

by Luna-Nanette

Speak to the moon, the sun, and the stars
Banish the fears, heal all the scars
Whisper a wish up to the sky
A wish for true love, a love that will never die.
And with the kiss, let the enchantment begin
A kiss blown through time that travels across space
A kiss that will light upon my true love's face.

— DESCRIPTION —

This simple spell will reveal a person's true love to him or her.

— SPELL —

1. Think about what attributes your true love should possess: specific looks, talent, or knowledge.
2. Recite the incantation, preferably outdoors in a quiet place under a starry sky.
3. After the incantation, blow a kiss into the wind.

✶ Wizard Persona ✶

Luna-Nanette has been writing since she was a child. She mainly writes poetry and short stories. Luna-Nanette currently lives a quiet, reclusive life in Groves, Texas.

The Unbreakable Bond Spell

by Rubiana Miene

— SPELL INCANTATION —

"Aevus adstrictus"

— DESCRIPTION —

This spell binds irrevocably two persons together for life. Once bound, neither person can harm the other. Furthermore, the two can communicate telepathically when in close proximity. In these communications, neither person can lie.

The spell was created for the purpose of marriage.

— SPELL —

The two people must cast the spell simultaneously, saying the words "Aevus adstrictus" three times with their wands pointed at each other. Each must not only focus on joining the other, but be sincerely intent on bonding; otherwise, the spell will fail.

A successful bonding results in a ring of white light enclosing the couple.

★ Wizard Persona ★

Rubiana Miene is a graduate of the Salem Academy and scholar of Magical Law. She presently resides in Berkeley, California and holds the position of Judge of Wizarding Family Court for the Northern District.

Practical
SPELLS

The Body Healing Spell
by Hephaistion

— SPELL INCANTATION —
"Vigoratus somes"

— DESCRIPTION —
This spell is used to heal the body of someone afflicted with disease. In addition to a wand, you will need a fireproof container, dried Hyssop, and a picture of the person you wish to heal.

— SPELL —

1. Burn a small amount of Hyssop in a fireproof container.
2. Takes the Hyssop ashes and rub them over your wand.
3. Grasp your wand in both hands and hold it over the picture of the afflicted person.
4. Move the wand clockwise and speak the incantation, "Vigoratus somes!"
5. After the incantation is spoken, wrap the picture in a white cloth.
6. Store the picture in a safe place.
7. Scatter the remaining ashes outdoors.

⋆ Wizard Persona ⋆

Hephaistion specializes in healing magic. He currently lives in southern California and offers his services to all those who seek him out.

The Healing Spell
by Kristela Kay Wishtend

— SPELL INCANTATION —

"Sun, moon, stars, and forces of light, may my [cite injured spot] please be all right."

— DESCRIPTION —

This spell removes aches and pains.

Caution: Use this only if you have an annoying or serious cramp, ache, pain, etc.

— SPELL —

Place your hand on or above the body part in pain and say the spell, "Sun, moon, stars, and forces of light, may my [cite injured spot] please be all right." Try not to think about that particular spot for the rest of the day.

✶ Wizard Persona ✶

Kristela Kay Wishtend once resided on her family's ancient British farm in Sussex near Tarberry Hill, from 1992–1997.

A Cleaning Spell
by Carson

— SPELL INCANTATION —
"Limpio"

— DESCRIPTION —

This simple spell can be used to clean efficiently and effectively all or part of your room.

— SPELL —

Point your wand at the part of your room that you want to clean and say, "Limpio."

— COUNTERSPELL —
"Messio"

⋆ Wizard Persona ⋆

Carson lives on a farm with fairies and goblins and has a pet dragon.

A Spell to Find Your Way
by Tangrene

— SPELL INCANTATION —
"Forken roadoso"

— DESCRIPTION —

This spell can be used when a young wizard is struggling with important decisions. It can be used to show the future and possible outcomes for various choices.

— SPELL —

Compose a mental picture of yourself and then use your wand and flick twice while saying the incantation, "Forken roadoso," to split your being into two entities.

.— NUANCES —

Imagine yourself where a road divides. Split your essence in two and send one down each path. They will return to the juncture where the road divides and tell you what lies ahead on their respective paths.

✴ Wizard Persona ✴

Tangrene provides counseling services for young wizards who have lost their way. She is often cited in *Wizarding Parent* and *The Educational Wizard Quarterly* for her controversial new thesis, "Bad Wizards are Bred, not Born."

A Spell to Lose Weight

by Professor Tanner

— SPELL INCANTATION —

"Weighto en lossouna"

— DESCRIPTION —

This simple spell makes you lose weight. There are no side effects.

— SPELL —

Think about being healthy. Place your wand on the area where you want to reduce your weight and gently wave your wand over it while speaking "Weighto en lossouna" four times.

✦ Wizard Persona ✦

Professor Tanner is the Deputy Headmaster at the Magic School. He is known for creating several health-related spells.

An Air Freshener Spell
by Auntie Tesa

— SPELL INCANTATION —
"Refreshum chambero"

— DESCRIPTION —
This spell will remove foul smells from a room.

— SPELL —
Hold your wand and make a circle; the bigger the room, the bigger the circle should be.

Concentrate on the odor you want to be present in the room (e.g., baking bread, cooking, vanilla, flowers, fresh mountain air).

⋆ Wizard Persona ⋆

Because **Auntie Tesa** suffered from allergies, as a child she was not allowed to have a cat, rat, or owl. This spell was created to help others with similar afflictions.

The "Learn While You Sleep" Spell

by Clarisse A. Storm

— SPELL INCANTATION —

"Literus osmosi"

— DESCRIPTION —

This spell downloads the contents of a book to your mind while you're sleeping.

— SPELL —

Before you go to bed, point your wand at the applicable book and say, "Literus osmosi." Place the book on top of your pillow and rest your head on the book.

★ Wizard Persona ★

Clarisse is a seer who works mostly with the Tarot cards. She is noted for her political predictions, having successfully predicted the winners of numerous elections.

The Problem-Ridding Spell
by Lexie

— SPELL INCANTATION —

"Alleviate"

— DESCRIPTION —

This spell is for girls who want to rid themselves of problems such as pimples, bad hair days, and the other afflictions.

— SPELL —

Think of the problem you want to fix and say, "Alleviate."

Read in the Dark Spell

by Paige Grimmer

— SPELL INCANTATION —

"Litari illuminey"

— DESCRIPTION —

When you are a child and have no candles, or want to do some secret reading at night after bedtime, use this spell to make the words in a book light up so you can read in the dark.

— SPELL —

Hold the book in your left hand. With your right hand, run your fingers over the cover and softly say, "Litari illuminey."

— COUNTERSPELL —

Close the book and blow across the cover as if you were blowing out a candle.

✶ Wizard Persona ✶

Grimmer has spent the last few years in Ireland, gathering local folklore and studying the habits of unicorns. She hopes to eventually publish a book on each subject.

The Alarm Clock Spell

by Deborah Hoad

— SPELL INCANTATION —

"Excito articulus singularis"

— DESCRIPTION —

Never sleep late again! This spell sets a magical alarm that will hover by your bedside to help you awake at the precise moment you've chosen.

The spell will work only for the wizard who conjures it. If, however, you want to wake up a room of people, use the plural form of the spell (singular: "Excito articulus singularis"; plural: "Excito articulus plura").

— SPELL —

State the words of the spell firmly as you draw a circle in the air with your wand in a counterclockwise motion. A thin gold circle will appear in the air. Write in the circle the time you want to wake up, and tap the top of the circle to set the alarm.

If the spell is not cast correctly, the conjured circle will disappear within two minutes. But if it's still visible after two minutes, the spell is properly set and you can lay your head down and sleep easy, knowing the spell will let you rest . . . for a spell.

— COUNTERSPELL —

Use any simple vanishing spell.

⋆ Wizard Persona ⋆

Deborah Hoad lives on the chilly Inner Wastelandia plateau, where her translations of ancient faerie scrolls have helped cure several types of jealousy warts.

The Beauty Spell
by Professor Lady Leaf

— SPELL INCANTATION —

"Mirror, mirror, look at me. Allow me to show off the face that I want them to see."

— DESCRIPTION —

This spell is frequently used by men and women who want to hide unsightly blemishes, dark circles under the eyes, aging lines—or just for fun (for example, to change eye color). The spell takes only ten minutes in front of a mirror. Also, because it lasts for a few hours, there's no need for a reversal spell.

— SPELL —

1. Stand in front of a mirror. Collect your thoughts and energy on the image of your face before you visualize what you would like changed or hidden.
2. Say, "Mirror, mirror, look at me. Allow me to show off the face that I want them to see."
3. Cup your hands over your face and concentrate on the changes that you want to occur.
4. Repeat until you feel your eyes become filmy. Look at your reflection and you'll see the change.

✴ Wizard Persona ✴

Professor Lady Leaf says, "I come from a long line of witches from various parts of Europe. The earliest account dates back to the fifth century B.C., in Druid, Ireland. I have been reborn many times. In my present life, I am a teacher of herbs, spells, and spirit communication."

The Cleaning Spell
by Luna Moniqua

— SPELL INCANTATION —
"Voco proluo prolutuon"

— DESCRIPTION —

This spell can be used to clean anything. It is used mostly by teenage witches and wizards to clean their rooms when their parents are nagging them about it.

— SPELL —

Swish and flick the wand and say, "Voco proluo prolutuon."

⭑ Wizard Persona ⭑

Luna, who lives in the U.K., sells cats and owls.

The Dream Spell
by Lee Carter

— SPELL INCANTATION —

"Dremeras advain"

— DESCRIPTION —

This spell prevents nightmares.

— SPELL —

Tap your pillow lightly with your wand four times and say the spell slowly, "Dremeras advain."

— COUNTERSPELL —

"Natouray retunas" will restore your natural dream cycle.

✴ Wizard Persona ✴

Lee Carter has been writing since age six. Born in England but currently living in the U.S., she plans on eventually returning to England. She currently writes about undiscovered creatures like the Endruffle.

The Easy Writing Spell
by Grammaria Matildakatt

— SPELL INCANTATION —
"Securus stilus"

— DESCRIPTION —

This spell can instantly fill out forms, applications, and other paperwork.

— SPELL —

This spell can be spoken, hummed, or imagined. Tap the wand twice on the document that must be completed. (Note: It is considered bad form to use this spell during exams, especially Wizzeen-Bingo matches, and at the dinner table.)

— COUNTERSPELL —

"Subsisto stilus ahora" (translation: Stop writing now!)

✷ Wizard Persona ✷

Professor Grammaria Matildakatt teaches Advanced Language Arts and routinely terrorizes her students with tons of homework related to an obscure but powerful branch of advanced magic known as *Scripsi-Universitas* (translation: College Writing, "To Write the Whole"/Universal Writing). With her fierce red-inked writing quill and her trademark sneer, she is loathed by students with a passion usually reserved for algebra teachers, drill sergeants, and potions instructors.

The Finding Spell

by Lilla Filosofo

— SPELL INCANTATION —

"Invenio"

— DESCRIPTION —

This spell leads you to lost things by using your wand like a diving-rod. For example, saying "invenio car keys" will lead you unerringly to your misplaced car keys.

— SPELL —

Hold the wand straight out in front of you and slowly move it back and forth as you say the spell. Follow the gentle tugging on the wand. (As you get closer to the lost item, the tugging sensation will become proportionally stronger.)

⋆ Wizard Persona ⋆

Lilla Filosofo is a sixteenth century Italian witch known for her creative nature. A fan of Da Vinci's works, Lilla lives in Venice, California and often visits the court of Queen Elizabeth I. (She is also rather messy and often misplaces things.)

The Fire-Making Spell

by Sanara

— SPELL INCANTATION —
"Lermyt fayar"

— DESCRIPTION —
This spell is used to light a candle or campfire. When used, the wand acts like a lighter, producing a small flame on its end.

— SPELL —
When performing this spell, swish your wand counterclockwise 180 degrees.

— COUNTERSPELL —
"Puirti cyth"

⋆ Wizard Persona ⋆

Sanara is a successful dragon breeder from Greenland. She is currently writing a book on how to handle dragon eggs properly. Sanara also has five dogs and three cats.

The Font-Changing Spell
by Professor John Haley

— SPELL INCANTATION —
"Abeo"

— DESCRIPTION —

This spell changes your text font, whether handwritten or computerized. You can make your font neater, messier, cooler, stranger, thinner, or bolder.

— SPELL —

Concentrate on the font attributes you want and wave your wand three times over the writing.

⋆ Wizard Persona ⋆

Professor John Haley invented Snapping Toffee, candy that snaps in your mouth. He taught at Minnesota Magic for five years.

The Forget-Me-Not Spell

by Amun

— SPELL INCANTATION —

"Memoria"

— DESCRIPTION —

This spell helps you remember a person's name and can be used in everyday circumstances.

— SPELL —

Picture the person's face in your mind and say the incantation, "Memoria."

★ Wizard Persona ★

Amun, who currently lives in Egypt, is credited with helping control the mummy population.

The Hair Growth Spell

by Rapunzel Pompadour

— SPELL INCANTATION —
"Folliculos fecundosious"

— DESCRIPTION —

This spell is used to produce thicker, more luxuriant hair. It can also be used to cure premature balding or reverse hair damage.

Caution: If the hair begins to show vine-like tendencies, call a botanist immediately. Do *not* approach with shears—the results could be fatal!

— SPELL —

Use your wand and gently tap the area where thicker hair is desired and speak the incantation, "Folliculos fecundosious."

★ Wizard Persona ★

Ms. Pompadour is the proprietress of The Enchantress, a beauty salon in Paramus, New Jersey.

The Hair Repair Spell

by Olivia Wenshoft

— SPELL INCANTATION —

"Extendamendo"

— DESCRIPTION —

If you get your hair cut short and don't like it, you can restore it to how it looked before the cut. For example, if a person who is not your friend catches you sleeping and takes a pair of scissors to cut off one of your ponytails, you can use this spell to restore the ponytail to its original state.

— SPELL —

Imagine your hair the way it was before the cut or the way you want it to be. Hold the wand in your left hand, gently tap once on your forefinger, and say, "Extendamendo."

★ Wizard Persona ★

Olivia Wenshoft comes from a long line of servants that have served the royal family of Torshaven since 1706. Olivia is the first in her family to attend college.

The Handwriting Helper Spell

by Esmeralda Valis

— SPELL INCANTATION —
"Decoro scripsi"

— DESCRIPTION —

This simple spell is used to make one's writing more visually appealing. It can be used to decorate invitations or personal letters, or to polish up an assignment before it's turned in. This spell is often used on diplomas and other official documents.

— SPELL —

1. Concentrate on the type of embellishment desired (for example, cursive script or animated text).
2. Run your wand down the length of the paper and say the incantation.

✷ Wizard Persona ✷

Valis graduated with dual degrees in Latin and Dragonology from the Wizarding Institute of Technology at Cambrian Hills (W.I.T.C.H.). She now divides her time between Dark Arts research in Romania and her budding dragon farm. Valis spends her free time researching and creating spells.

The Holding Spell
by Garfonius

— SPELL INCANTATION —
"Shoperlo"

— DESCRIPTION —
This simple but useful spell frees your hands of holding shopping bags so you can shop in comfort.

— SPELL —
Say, "Shoperlo," and all of your purchased items will levitate and trail behind you as you continue to shop.

— COUNTERSPELL —
"Groundento"

✴ Wizard Persona ✴
Garfonius is a beautiful witch who loves flying her broom to the mall to shop.

The Kneading Spell

by Professor Ant

— SPELL INCANTATION —

"Knead"

— DESCRIPTION —

Intended for kneading dough in classic bread making, this spell frees up the wizard chef to look after other food in the kitchen.

— SPELL —

Massage your fingers in the air while saying the incantation, "Knead." (The longer you need to knead the dough, the longer you should massage your fingers in the air.)

✶ Wizard Persona ✶

Professor Ant teaches cooking classes at the Toadstool Academy of Culinary Arts in Thorny Hill, Canada. She competed in the National Cook-Off in 2006 and won top honors for her Pumpkin Praline Pancake, now a breakfast favorite.

The Meal Preparation Spell
by Victula DuJour

"Victus preparo"

— DESCRIPTION —

This spell summons a meal for hungry wizards who don't know how to cook. It's handy when away from home, but even handier when you have unexpected company!

— SPELL —

Think about what you want to eat and wave your wand in a stirring or whisking motion and say, "Victus preparo."

✶ Wizard Persona ✶

Victula DuJour is the original wizard chef! She has created menus for many magical people and hopes to become famous for her recipes.

The Mixing Spell

by Briana Salcedo

— SPELL INCANTATION —
"Miscere"

— DESCRIPTION —

This spell can only be used with properties that could be manually mixed. (For example, you cannot mix a block of lead with sand.) This spell is typically used in simpler potions, cooking, and paint blending.

— SPELL —

Put the items to be mixed in a single container. Imagine what the solution should look like when mixed. Then, use your wand to make a circular motion over the container. With practice, you will be able to mix without spilling and also be able to control the mixing speed.

— COUNTERSPELL —
"Dividere"

★ Wizard Persona ★

Briana Salcedo is credited with her paintings of magical beasts, created with charms she discovered.

The Note-Taking Spell

by Elizabeth Luchko

— SPELL INCANTATION —

"Obtineo-lacuna"

— DESCRIPTION —

This spell makes your pen take notes for you in class.

— SPELL —

Point your wand at your pen and say, "Obtineo-lacuna."

— COUNTERSPELL —

"Exigo"

⋆ Wizard Persona ⋆

Elizabeth has been teaching witches and wizards since 1988. She is celebrated for her new teaching methods.

The Oak Memory Spell
by Greendragon

— SPELL INCANTATION —

"This is never to be forgotten! In memoriam, forget ye not!"

— DESCRIPTION —

The wise old oak tree has always been revered by witches, druids, and the like. An especially long-lived tree, a grand oak has seen several centuries pass. Its branches and leaves hold the reverberations of many lifetimes, which is why it is effective in memory spells. Remember, the leaves must be fallen leaves gathered from the ground. *Never* steal leaves from a living tree!

— SPELL —

1. Take seven fallen leaves from the oldest oak tree you can find in your area. (Remember to thank the tree after you have gathered the leaves. A hug always goes down well!)
2. Place the leaves in a small pan of spring water, collected at the source (though bottled water will do). Bring to a boil. Turn off the heat and let the leaves steep for seven minutes, during which time you can prepare the next part of the spell.
3. Take a strip of cloth (linen is best, but any will do) and with the tip of your wand, trace on the surface of the cloth that which you wish to remember: the word, phrase, or number sequence. Do this seven times, and then tap the cloth seven times while saying the incantation, "This is never to be forgotten! In memoriam, forget ye not!"

4. Immerse the cloth in the oak tea so that it is soaked. Squeeze out the cloth and lay it over your forehead as you lie back and relax. Stay like this with your eyes closed and focus for seven minutes on the thing you wish to remember.

Now, you will never forget that vital spell formula, history date, or whatever has been eluding your memory.

After performing the spell, the oak leaves and water should be emptied over a garden or anywhere outdoors where the leaves can decompose and return to nature.

The cloth can be rinsed out, dried, and kept to be used the next time you need an aide-memoire!

✴ Wizard Persona ✴

Greendragon is an "old style" witch, having learned the traditions of the ancient ways at one of the best schools in Britain. She is especially fond of poetical love spells and hopes one day to find the perfect warlock with whom to share her hobby of tinkering with vintage broomsticks.

The Parting Spell
by Arika

— SPELL INCANTATION —

"Agito absens"

— DESCRIPTION —

This is a spell that's especially useful when too many people are in front of you. It's also useful when you're driving to work.

— SPELL —

Make three clockwise turns with your wand, point in front of you, and say, "Agito absens." The foot traffic will then move to either side of you. After you walk by, the foot traffic goes back to normal. Nobody will know how or why the traffic parted or restored itself.

✳ Wizard Persona ✳

Arika is a young witch whose parents are Maglinots. She is an only child. She has a love of learning and enjoys school, where she has many friends.

The Perfect Temperature Spell
by Altrina

— SPELL INCANTATION —

"Excellente temperatarus"

— DESCRIPTION —

This spell is used to make whatever drink or food you wish to consume the perfect temperature.

— SPELL —

Point your wand at the drink or food which needs to be cooled or heated and say, "Excellente temperatarus."

✶ Wizard Persona ✶

Altrina is an apprentice at a care center for phoenixes.

The Plant-Reviving Spell

by Nicoletta Severene

— SPELL INCANTATION —

"Flora revivere"

— DESCRIPTION —

This is a simple household spell used to bring houseplants back from the edge of death. This spell is especially handy for the forgetful and for those who take long vacations.

— SPELL —

Stare directly at the plant and point your wand at its roots, flick the wand once, and say, "Flora revivere."

✶ Wizard Persona ✶

Nicoletta Severene was one of the first to combine botany and spells. Her work lead to the creation of the "aliquantus" strain of Flytrap. She currently lives in a very large greenhouse in Wales.

The Purification Spell

by Katrina Ilich

— SPELL INCANTATION —
"Defaeco"

— DESCRIPTION —
This spell purifies any liquid by removing all impurities, including toxins, bacteria, and poisons.

— SPELL —

1. Concentrate and wave your wand in a circular motion as if you were waving a stream of water out of the liquid you are casting upon and say, "Defaeco."
2. After completing the circular motion, jerk your wand back, pulling all unwanted impurities from the liquid.

✶ Wizard Persona ✶

Ms. Ilich is descended from Serbian and Russian ancestry, some linked to the royal family and also the famous potion maker, Gregor Nensvoski. She has been studying for eight years various magical liquids, potions, and poisons. A graduate of the University of Magical Fluids, she is now a member of the National Potions and Poisons Society. Two years ago, she created the Unda Spiritus potion that allows the user to breathe underwater.

The Self-Stitching Charm

by Alessandra Brinklebell

— SPELL INCANTATION —

"Sua sute"

— DESCRIPTION —

Ever find a tear in your dress robes just before a big social outing? Need to sew a hat together but don't want to risk pricking your fingers? Used for centuries, this charm has always been very popular among housewives. Once the charm is uttered, the seams in the cloth and other materials connect and stitch themselves together.

Caution: Don't let your mind wander using this spell as this may cause unintended consequences. For instance, if you let your mind stray to field mice, this spell could easily make your garment's thread resemble a furry tail!

— SPELL —

1. Wave your wand and point at the area that needs to be repaired and say, "Sua sute."
2. If you wish the stitches to be of a certain color, concentrate on that color as you speak the incantation.

— COUNTERSPELL —

A tearing, cutting, or separating charm all work . . . or use a pair of ordinary scissors.

★ Wizard Persona ★

A witch from the eighteenth century, **Alessandra** lives among Maglinot folk as a seamstress and clothier in London. Due to her "magically fast" production of garments, she became one of the most popular tailors in the city. She is credited with many charms and spells for the sewing profession.

The Unraveling Spell
by Gwendolyn Mortina

— SPELL INCANTATION —
"Fiberus unravelus"

— DESCRIPTION —
This spell will take apart any braids in hair or rope. It works on knots, too. The spell is occasionally used by sailors who need to untie knots on anchors or sails.

— SPELL —
Say, "Fiberus unravelus," and move your wand in a clockwise motion over the braid or knot until it has separated itself. The tighter the knot, though, the longer you will have to make a clockwise motion over it to untangle it.

⋆ Wizard Persona ⋆

Gwendolyn Mortina is a famous hairstylist known for all her hair-raising (and taming) spells. She is credited for making the first color-changing wig. She lives in New York City.

The Water Spell
by Ryan Christopher Fortner

— SPELL INCANTATION —
"Aqua jacio"

— DESCRIPTION —

This spell can squirt a stream of water, large or small, out from the wand tip at another person.

— SPELL —

Concentrate on the color mauve, flick your wand twice at the other person, and imagine him wet. (If you merely want to wet him down, think of a small amount of water. But if you want to drench him, think of a lot of water, like shooting out from a fire hose.)

— COUNTERSPELL —

"Aquivanasca"

✴ Wizard Persona ✴

Ryan crossbreeds dragons and has created a hybrid dragon, which is part Moke and part Peruvian Vipertoth.

The Writing Spell

by Professor Harrison

— SPELL INCANTATION —

"Que ah latoor"

— DESCRIPTION —

This spell will control your quill to write out all of your thoughts. It automatically spells words correctly and fixes your grammar and punctuation.

— SPELL —

Point your wand at the quill and say the incantation out loud, "Que ah latoor."

— COUNTERSPELL —

"Que ah latah"

⁕ Wizard Persona ⁕

Professor Harrison is currently a teacher at a southern California school for young witches and wizards. She enjoys teaching her eager students new spells and potions every week.

Time, Space, and
Weather Manipulation
SPELLS

Change the Weather Spell

by Twyla Ellastonia

"Elountous saetu"

— DESCRIPTION —

This spell can temporarily change the weather in a twenty-foot radius. For example, you can change the weather from rainy to sunny, thunderstorms to snowstorms. But if you try to use the spell to hurt someone, it will backfire.

— SPELL —

Visualize the weather and concentrate. The power and duration of the spell depends on how much you concentrate.

— COUNTERSPELL —

"Refot chetop"

⋆ Wizard Persona ⋆

Twyla is 75 percent human and 25 percent fairy. An excellent potions student and a passionate fairy lover, she lives in a castle in northern America. She enjoys reading, music, and writing. She likes to draw, hang out with her friends, loves to travel, and is always open for an adventure. Twyla loves all kinds of wizard candy.

The Self-Placement in Picture Spell

by Cynthia B.

— SPELL INCANTATION —

"Piceye"

— DESCRIPTION —

This spell allows the spell caster to enter a painting or picture and live within it.

Caution: Because there's no sense of the passage of time when living in the painted world, the danger is that you may stay longer than you intended—for hours, sometimes even days.

— SPELL —

The ingredients needed include hair from a unicorn tail, a wolf's tooth, and dragon spit.

Picture yourself in the picture, and then combine the three ingredients in a small cauldron. Stir briskly and repeat "Piceye" three times.

— COUNTERSPELL —

"Reverto"

✦ Wizard Persona ✦

Cynthia B. works with oil paintings and photographs to capture the real person within; thus, no secrets can be hidden from her camera or paintings.

The Slow Motion Spell

by Brittney Brown

— SPELL INCANTATION —

"Slugurtle"

— DESCRIPTION —

This spell makes everything in a room but you move in slow motion. This spell is especially useful if a spell is being used against you and you need to get out of its way.

— SPELL —

Think of a snail, twirl your wand over your head, and thrust your wand forward.

⋆ Wizard Persona ⋆

Brittney is currently practicing her skills as a chef. She resides in Vancouver, Washington.

The Specific Portal Spell
by Preussia

— SPELL INCANTATION —
"Portelulius"

— DESCRIPTION —

This is a spell that will take you wherever you want or to whomever you need to find. It's useful if you need to locate a lost person, go somewhere fast, or just get away.

— SPELL —

Point your wand at the tip of your nose, close your eyes, focus on the place you'd like to go or the person you'd like to go to, and say, "Portelulius."

Remember to be completely focused and specific on the place/person you wish to see/meet.

— COUNTERSPELL —

To get back to your starting point, concentrate on the place you want to return to, point your wand at the tip of your nose, close your eyes, and say, "Portelulius."

✦ Wizard Persona ✦

Preussia wants to work with magical creatures.

The Stealth Spell

by FrozenBliss

— SPELL INCANTATION —

"Evanui"

— DESCRIPTION —

This spell makes an object or a person disappear and then reappear in another place.

Caution: Be careful not to be distracted or sidetracked, or the object or person will end up where you don't want them to be.

— SPELL —

Concentrate on the object or person that you wish to disappear and think of where you want the object or person to reappear.

— COUNTERSPELL —

"Appareo"

✷ Wizard Persona ✷

FrozenBliss owns a book/candy shop. She created Camobits, a candy that camouflages. (The camouflage wears off once the candy is gone.)

The Thunderstorm Spell

by R. N. Rottwieller

— SPELL INCANTATION —

"Fretom petro blatrater sefortes"

— DESCRIPTION —

This spell will create a thunderstorm around anything you'd like to protect, like a house or castle. It is often used to ward off door-to-door solicitors or thieves.

— SPELL —

Stand on the highest point of the structure, raise both hands skyward, and say the spell, "Fretom petro blatrater sefortes," four times as loudly as you can.

— COUNTERSPELL —

Stand on the lowest point of the structure, lower both hands downward, and say, **"Setroffes valtartak ortep moterf."**

✴ Wizard Persona ✴

Rottwieller lives on a flying stingray named Nimbulosirus.

The Time-Pausing Spell

by Merlinia Roeluna

— SPELL INCANTATION —
"Glacia timus"

— DESCRIPTION —

This spell will pause time for up to ten minutes. It's most commonly used to prevent spills or to keep a person from falling.

— SPELL —

Make two clockwise turns with your wand and say, "Glacia timus."

✷ Wizard Persona ✷

Merlinia is famous for defeating a rogue troll. She will soon be graduating from wizardry school.

The Time-Rewinding Spell

by Lucas Ansell

— SPELL INCANTATION —
"Rewindus unhourus"

— DESCRIPTION —

This spell allows you to turn back time one hour, giving you time to undo previous mistakes.

— SPELL —

Point your wand at the hands of a clock and direct the hand back one hour as you say the incantation, "Rewindus unhourus."

✦ Wizard Persona ✦

Lucas lives with 47 cats, five snakes, one scorpion, and his brother Nicholas, who is a wizard. When Lucas is not practicing spells, he writes mystery novels about witches.

The Time-Stopping Spell

by Erago

— SPELL INCANTATION —

"Freezious"

— DESCRIPTION —

This spell will freeze time. This spell can be used at any time, but it's best used to escape from your enemy during combat. It's also useful in evading attacks from dragons and other malevolent, magical creatures.

— SPELL —

Only a powerful wizard can perform this spell. Point your wand skyward, imagine a frozen world, and say, "Freezious."

— COUNTERSPELL —

"Brisinger"

★ Wizard Persona ★

Erago is a young wizard seeking fame and fortune. He has created many spells that are especially useful when working outside with magical creatures.

Time Travel Spell

by Frankie Ruby

— SPELL INCANTATION —
"Tempus temporis eo ireitum"

— DESCRIPTION —
This spell will take you to the date and time that you say or think. The spell can only be used by the person who casts the spell. During time travel, you are invisible and only an observer. Such a spell is especially helpful if you've lost something and need to go back in the past to find out where you left it.

— SPELL —
When casting the spell, think of your favorite color as you close your eyes, and do the chicken dance.

— COUNTERSPELL —
To get back to the present, say the spell backwards: **"Ireitum eo temporis tempus."**

The Window-Walking Spell

by Madame Carole Conner Davis

— SPELL INCANTATION —

"Intro speculum"

— DESCRIPTION —

This is an advanced spell used to make a mirror that acts as a door to another place. Stepping through the mirror to another location is commonly called "window walking," similar to climbing through an open window. This spell is commonly used when a person needs to be able to travel to another place on a regular basis.

— SPELL —

Say "Intro speculum" and send an object through the mirror to the predesignated location. This creates a pathway. The "window" remains open until the counterspell is used to close the window.

— NUANCES —

Concentrate heavily on the location as you speak the spell.

— COUNTERSPELL —

"Propinquus"

✴ Wizard Persona ✴

Madame Davis is a potion and spell creator. She is the author of *Wizard Chronicles*, a genealogical guide to the more common surnames in wizarding history.

Dueling
SPELLS

The Bubble Prison Curse

by Giomanch Huntro

— SPELL INCANTATION —
"Inkarosa"

— DESCRIPTION —
This curse traps your opponent in a large, golden, unbreakable bubble. This spell could be used to immobilize your opponent and is especially useful when dueling.

— SPELL —
Think of loneliness, and with your wand, cross from your left shoulder to your right hip, and then over your head and point at your opponent while saying the incantation.

— COUNTERSPELL —
"Intercessorus"

★ Wizard Persona ★

Giomanch is in his fifth year as a student at Gondrac's Academy for Gifted American Wizards (class of 2012). He is most noted for having the highest score on his National Wizarding Examination. Upon graduation, he hopes to be selected for the Committee for Creation of Spells and Charms.

The Bubble Spell
by Epona

— SPELL INCANTATION —

"Ebullio sursum"

— DESCRIPTION —

This spell makes the victim spout bubbles out of his mouth when-ever opened. It's great for dueling because it makes the opponent unable to speak spells. It's also good for use against people who can't keep secrets or rumors.

— SPELL —

Make a circle with your wand and flick once. Concentrate on the spell and say, "Ebullio sursum." The more you concentrate, the longer the spell lasts.

✷ Wizard Persona ✷

Epona grew up not knowing she is a witch. Her parents are Maglinots. She uses reiki and herbology, as well as other healing arts with her creatures.

The Camouflage Spell

by Colesta

— SPELL INCANTATION —

"Camedecepto"

— DESCRIPTION —

This quick spell can be used to make the spell caster blend into his surrounding environment. It's useful for spying and to avoid detection when in places you're not supposed to be.

Note: This spell must be practiced to perfect confidence. If the spell is not spoken with confidence, you could end up only partially camouflaged.

— SPELL —

Speak the incantation, "Camedecepto."

— COUNTERSPELL —

"Camerevelo"

★ Wizard Persona ★

Colesta breeds magical dogs for witches and wizards.

The Disarming Spell

by Molly Cahill

— SPELL INCANTATION —

"Prosnake!"

— DESCRIPTION —

This spell is used to disarm anyone you wish. It's most commonly used in wizard duels.

— SPELL —

Point your wand at the person, keep steady eye contact, and say, "Prosnake!"

⋆ Wizard Persona ⋆

Molly hides her magical powers so others won't use her to solve their own problems.

The "Dragon Reflection" Spell
by Greg of Griffin

— SPELL INCANTATION —
"Dracosec reflecta"

— DESCRIPTION —

This is a very powerful defensive spell normally used by dark wizards. The spell is generally used only in dire circumstances or when the wizard anticipates a very strong attack. It is capable of repelling essentially any curse or spell cast when it is in force. The spell requires a high level of skill and a tremendous amount of energy. As a result, very few wizards can maintain it for more than thirty seconds.

— SPELL —

1. Draw yourself up to full height and extend both arms in a winglike pattern.
2. With a loud, strong voice say, "Dracosec reflecta."

✶ Wizard Persona ✶

Greg of Griffin has traveled the world as a well-known healer. He has enjoyed positions as the official healer of many royal courts.

The Fog Spell

by Jessica Culwell

— SPELL INCANTATION —

"Nebula"

— DESCRIPTION —

This simple spell creates a thick fog so you can create a distraction or escape undercover.

— SPELL —

Think of a fog and say, "Nebula."

— COUNTERSPELL —

"Apricus nebula"

★ Wizard Persona ★

Jessica is a 13-year-old autodidact who currently lives in Corona, California. She enjoys reading, dancing, and spending time with friends.

The Hallucination Spell

by Angel Darkfield

— SPELL INCANTATION —
"Noisullio"

— DESCRIPTION —
This spell causes your opponent to have illusions or hallucinations. It is most often used during duels.

— SPELL —
Take a deep breath, point your wand at your opponent, and say, "Noisullio."

— COUNTERSPELL —
"De-noisullio"

✶ Wizard Persona ✶
Angel has been in hiding for the past five years. She is best known for her psychic powers.

The Hand Magic Spell
by Ashley Grey

— SPELL INCANTATION —

"Hanmagico"

— DESCRIPTION —

This spell allows you to use your hands in place of a wand to counter curses, hexes, and countercurses. You can perform any magic using your hands with this spell, "Hanmagico."

— SPELL —

Loosely hold your wand in one hand and pretend you're holding a wand in your other hand. Look at your hands and say, "Hanmagico." Your hands should glow a light blue. Once the blue light has faded, you can perform magic with your hands.

— COUNTERSPELL —

"Hanmagif"

★ Wizard Persona ★

Ashley Grey is very adventurous and loves researching magical creatures.

The Invisible Bug Spell

by Heather McNilly

— SPELL INCANTATION —

"Insecto inviseeblo"

— DESCRIPTION —

This is a good distraction spell. Use this spell to create the feeling of being covered in tiny, crawly bugs. Of course, there are no bugs, but it will cause the afflicted person to feel tiny bugs running all over them. It is especially effective in creating an elevated sense of paranoia.

— SPELL —

Before conducting this spell, the spell caster should ask, "Is that a bug on your shoulder?" Follow this up quickly by pressing four fingers from each hand together, so that you have eight fingers (like a spider's eight legs) touching tip to tip in a prayer-like manner. Quietly murmur the incantation, "Insecto inviseeblo."

— COUNTERSPELL —

Should you find yourself "covered" in small bugs that you cannot see or get rid of, stomp your left foot on the ground and say, **"Squashious perfectus,"** to make the sensation go away.

★ Wizard Persona ★

Ms. McNilly leads a quiet life, and has lived in a tree for the last seventeen years, attempting to commune with the local Birch Sprites and hoping to learn their well-guarded cure for the common cold.

WHIMSIC ALLEY

Whimsic Alley
Fine Shops

Since
1367

2717 ½ Wilshire Blvd.
Santa Monica, CA 90403
www.WhimsicAlley.com

Habber & Dasher, located on Whimsic Alley, is one of the world's few suppliers of adult and youth gaming sweaters. Gaming robes are expected in the near future.

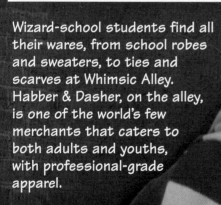

Wizard-school students find all their wares, from school robes and sweaters, to ties and scarves at Whimsic Alley. Habber & Dasher, on the alley, is one of the world's few merchants that caters to both adults and youths, with professional-grade apparel.

A wizard's wand is his most powerful and versatile tool. Therefore wizards always have theirs with them. Any well-made robe, such as the ones sold by Habber & Dasher on Whimsic Alley, will include an interior wand pocket.

Student wizards arrive at
school not only dressed
appropriately but with
all the necessary accou-
trements, including
feather quills, leather
journals, seals, wizard
books, and wands.
These students found
everything they needed
at the shops along
Whimsic Alley.

Old world shopping elegance is what one finds at Whimsic Alley. From Widdleshaft's Quill & Ink shop to the Phoenix Wands shop, even Maglinots will feel they have been transported to another era.

The selection of his wand is one of the earliest and most important decisions a wizard will ever make. Phoenix Wands has been making wands since 437 B.C. and offers a variety to please even the fussiest wizard.

Widdleshaft's Quill &
Ink shop features a
wide assortment of
feather quills, writing
and drawing journals,
seals, parchment, and
writing accessories.

Across the alley, the HP Wizard Store,
boasts the world's largest assortment
of Harry Potter–brand merchandise.

Sensible wizards avoid confrontation with those who practice the dark arts, yet they are always at the ready. Selecting the right wand, always having it with you, and mastering the proper spells are key elements in your defense against
the dark arts.

The Nightmare Spell
by Lady Evil

— SPELL INCANTATION —
"Oculus infernum"

— DESCRIPTION —

This spell causes its victim to have the most frightening night-mares. They will see what is to them purgatory. It should be used with extreme caution and only by experienced spell casters.

— SPELL —

You must be extremely angry at the time you want to cast the spell. Point your wand at the victim and hold it as still as possible.

★ Wizard Persona ★

Lady Evil has long been known for her love of all things dark and evil. She currently lives in the Midwest and plans for the day when she can take over the world.

The Phobia Spell

by Esmeralda Eversole

— SPELL INCANTATION —

"Ostendo sum vereor!"

— DESCRIPTION —

This spell shows a person's deepest fear and makes it appear before your opponent.

— SPELL —

Speak, "Ostendo sum vereor!"

— NUANCES —

You must either be in great danger or fear for your life in order for this spell to work.

⋆ Wizard Persona ⋆

Esmeralda lives in the Appalachian mountains of West Virginia. She and her husband raise a household magical creature.

The Protection Spell

by Alexandria Moonberry

— SPELL INCANTATION —

"Contego"

— DESCRIPTION —

This spell casts an aura around the spell caster or around the person the spell caster wishes, making one untouchable and protected from harm.

This is an extremely powerful spell and should be used only by accomplished witches and wizards.

— SPELL —

Concentrate on creating a sphere around yourself or the person you wish to protect and say, "Contego."

★ Wizard Persona ★

Alexandria was born in Egypt but raised in Romania. Currently residing in London, she can frequently be found in Cairo. She's best known for creating spells and her work with dragons.

The Rubber Charm
by Cilla Atia

— SPELL INCANTATION —
"Rubberious!"

— DESCRIPTION —

This charm causes the spell caster's skin to become rubberlike in texture, yielding protection against many jinxes and curses.

Caution: Do not try to walk or move much when under this spell because you will wiggle to the point of motion sickness!

— SPELL —

Say, "Rubberious!"

— NUANCES —

Do not cast this charm on a full stomach. You may experience slight nausea when returning to a solid state.

— COUNTERSPELL —

This charm can be ended by using the **"Cementious"** charm, which temporarily turns the person into a statue.

✶ Wizard Persona ✶

A witch who has the handy gift of absorption, **Cilla** is at work on spells and charms to ward off some jinxes.

The "See Yourself" Spell

by Meike Zane

— SPELL INCANTATION —

"Appearium reflectum"

— DESCRIPTION —

With this spell, your reflection will appear in the air in front of you. It's quite useful if you are in urgent need of a mirror.

— SPELL —

While saying the spell, draw the outline of a circle and point in its middle with your wand.

— COUNTERSPELL —

Walk through the air where the reflection is to make it disappear.

★ Wizard Persona ★

Meike has lived in her adorable cottage in Elsloo, the Netherlands, since 1990. She is the inventor of this spell, which has been useful to witches and wizards worldwide.

The Spell of Forgetfulness

by Maery

— SPELL INCANTATION —

"Demen zione"

— DESCRIPTION —

This spell makes your opponent or victim forget what he was about to do. You could possibly use this spell on a teacher who is just about to give you a pop quiz or if you have just been grounded by your parents.

— SPELL —

Wave your wand back and forth, and then pull it back and jab forward toward the victim and say, "Demen zione."

✴ Wizard Persona ✴

Maery tracks and observes unicorn trails and animal behavior. She is also known as the creator of the Uni Tail Shampoo, which keeps human hair as silky as a unicorn's tail.

The Spell of Wise Silence
by Ivy

— SPELL INCANTATION —
"Sophotacetus"

— DESCRIPTION —

This spell is cast when you want to prevent yourself or someone else from saying something that would hurt another person's feelings or to reveal something that should be kept secret.

— SPELL —

If you have a feeling that it would be best to be guarded in your comments prior to a sticky situation, point your wand tip at the throat of the individual who you wish to refrain from saying hurtful things and say, "Sophotacetus."

✶ Wizard Persona ✶

Ivy is a healer who can transform herself into an owl and fly to witches and wizards who need her help.

The Spell to Cast a Quick Shadow

by Britannia Cirindë-Bramblerose
Moonsire Falconheart

— SPELL INCANTATION —

"Partum umbra"

— DESCRIPTION —

This spell creates a sphere of shadows to surround another person.
It distracts the person as long as the spell caster can keep the spell
active.

— SPELL —

Hold out your dominant hand, concentrate on a dark sphere, and
say, "Partum umbra."

— COUNTERSPELL —

"Sol contego" (sun shield) which creates a bright halo of light.

⋆ Wizard Persona ⋆

Britannia is a New England sorceress who uses older magic
that few people have the ability to wield. Her aim is to cause distrac-
tions for those who need them. Though originally from
Massachusetts, Britannia currently resides in Vermont.

The Spell to Create Webbing

by Professor Morrison

— SPELL INCANTATION —

"Webthesis"

— DESCRIPTION —

This spell produces thick, ropy webbing out of your wand. This spell is useful for ensnaring your opponent.

— SPELL —

Point your wand at your opponent and say, "Webthesis."

⋆ Wizard Persona ⋆

Professor Morrison is best known for creating spells.

The Stumbling Spell

by Joel Susaya

— SPELL INCANTATION —

"Lubricugum"

— DESCRIPTION —

This spell causes a person's feet to lose friction, causing him to perpetually slip and stumble, but without actually falling. This makes it difficult for the victim to cast a spell.

— SPELL —

1. Concentrate on something wet and slippery.
2. With your wand, make two clockwise rotations and say, "Lubricugum," and aim your wand at the victim's feet.

— COUNTERSPELL —

Focus on something dry and make two counterclockwise rotations. Say, "Institietum," and aim your wand at the victim's feet.

⋆ Wizard Persona ⋆

Joel is an up-and-coming wizard with great potential and unlimited imagination, useful for many varieties of spells.

The Tinnitus Spell
by Madame C. Conner Davis

— SPELL INCANTATION —
"Auris tinnio"

— DESCRIPTION —

This spell makes a person have a loud, annoying ringing sensation in his ears. It is used to distract, annoy, or cause someone not to be able to hear clearly.

— SPELL —

Point your wand at the victim and say, "Auris tinnio."

— COUNTERSPELL —
"Abrogo tinnio"

✴ Wizard Persona ✴

Madame Davis is a potions and spell designer. The author of *Wizard Chronicles*, she is currently working on a fantasy novel.

The Verbal Paralyzing Spell

by Rachael Phillips

— SPELL INCANTATION —

"Paralycium verbatum"

— DESCRIPTION —

This spell causes the victim to not be able to speak for five minutes.

— SPELL —

Use your wand to swish and flick, and then aim straight at the victim's mouth.

✶ Wizard Persona ✶

Rachael currently owns a potions ingredient store near her cottage in Wisconsin.

Communication
SPELLS

A Charm to Translate an Infant's Crying

by Ashley Hilton

— SPELL INCANTATION —

"Incylantantis"

— DESCRIPTION —

This charm translates the cry of a baby into understandable words. Parents would use it on their children to quickly understand what they are crying about to aid in the process of helping the children efficiently and effectively.

— SPELL —

Trace the baby's mouth in a clockwise motion with the wand and concentrate on his cries.

— COUNTERSPELL —

Trace the baby's mouth with the wand in a counterclockwise motion and say, **"Subsisto."**

A Spell to Reveal Memories

by Madison Walker

— SPELL INCANTATION —

"Memorala"

— DESCRIPTION —

This spell allows a person to bring up memories or see memories from another person's mind. This is especially useful in trial cases when the accused refuses to talk.

— SPELL —

You must look directly into the person's eyes and not blink for three seconds. You must know also what you are looking for. Then whisper the incantation, "Memorala," and vivid memories will be extracted from the other person's mind.

✴ Wizard Persona ✴

Madison Walker has studied potions since the age of five. She is best known for her creation of the "Glaserious" potion, which is used to make any object transparent.

The Animal Language Spell

by Crystal Moonstar

— SPELL INCANTATION —

"Lingua bestia"

— DESCRIPTION —

This spell allows the caster to communicate for one hour with any creature (Magique or Maglinot). This spell is particularly useful when engaging creatures who do not speak a language humans can understand.

Caution: This spell will *not* guarantee that a hostile creature will not attack.

— SPELL —

Point your wand at the creature, flick once, and state the incantation, "Lingua bestia."

✶ Wizard Persona ✶

Miss Crystal Moonstar is responsible for one of the few winged unicorn preserves in the world. She has also published *Winged Unicorns: Lost Wonders*, in which she discusses their near extinction. She currently lives on a preserve in remote Europe.

The Fluency Spell
by Dragonestra

— SPELL INCANTATION —
"Polyglotus"

— DESCRIPTION —
This spell allows the user to become fluent in all languages at once.

— SPELL —
Point your wand at your throat, rotate it counterclockwise three times, and say, "Polyglotus." If the language you wish to speak is signed, point your wand at you hand instead of your throat.

— NUANCES —
You won't be able to use a language until someone first speaks to you in it. If you need to be the first one to speak, concentrate on the specific language as you say the spell.

— COUNTERSPELL —
"Uniglotus"

✷ Wizard Persona ✷

Dragonestra lives in the high reaches of the Himalayas, where she raises and trains the rare white abominable snowdragon. Unfortunately, she doesn't get out much, so this spell is of very little use to her.

The Revealing Spell

by Beater #1

— SPELL INCANTATION —

"Insimartae attritus"

— DESCRIPTION —

This spell tells you what's inside an object. For instance, if you want to know what's inside your friend's bag, say the spell and his bag will become temporarily transparent.

— SPELL —

Use your wand to touch the object you wish to look into and say, "Insimartae attritus."

— COUNTERSPELL —

"Kasaero"

✴ Wizard Persona ✴

Beater #1 is currently studying the habits of mermaids in the wild.

The Silencing Spell
by Nibellus Gutenberg

— SPELL INCANTATION —
"Silentus"

— DESCRIPTION —

This spell is used in situations when someone is talking too much but has nothing worthwhile to say. It leaves the victim in total silence and with a cold feeling in his throat that can be removed by the spell caster only.

— SPELL —

Just say, "Silentus."

— COUNTERSPELL —
"Tellibento"

★ Wizard Persona ★

Nibellus is best known for his sound-making inventions, the Paraphone and the Mega-High Voicer, which were so popular that he left his native Russia to live in the Caribbean.

The Talking Animal Spell

by Melcy Rine

— SPELL INCANTATION —
"Sermo animalia: English"

— DESCRIPTION —
This spell gives an animal the power to speak English or, if desired, another language.

— SPELL —
With the tip of your wand, tap the animal twice on its head and say, "Sermo animalia: English." (If a language other than English is desired, substitute its name instead.)

— COUNTERSPELL —
"Silentium animalia"

⋆ Wizard Persona ⋆
Melcy is a lifelong resident of Edinburgh, Scotland. She is best known for inventing Amazing Talking Animal Crackers, which she produces in her factory for sale to witches and wizards everywhere.

The Tongue Translator

by Ali Corium

— SPELL INCANTATION —

"Lingua interpretate"

— DESCRIPTION —

This spell translates foreign tongues into a language comprehensible by the spell caster.

The spell is extremely useful when traveling abroad. For example, it can be used in crowded Middle Eastern markets when you wish to understand what the merchant is saying, or in French coffee shops when you suspect the locals are prone to gossip about the fashion sense (or lack thereof) of tourists.

— SPELL —

Concentrate upon the tongue of the person and say, "Lingua interpretate."

— COUNTERSPELL —

"Impedimentum interpretatis"

✴ Wizard Persona ✴

Ali Corium is best known for her design of a magical theme park for Maglinots. She studied wizardry in France before becoming a professor at a private school of wizardry in the U.S.

Miscellany
SPELLS

The Automatic Drawing Spell

by Ryan Christopher Fortner

— SPELL INCANTATION —

"Artisco"

— DESCRIPTION —

This spell can draw anything you want.

— SPELL —

Use your wand to draw four vertical lines and one horizontal line.
The spell will draw what you imagined on any surface you point to.

— COUNTERSPELL —

"Eraisofy"

✴ Wizard Persona ✴

Ryan crosses magical animals to create new breeds.

The Balancing Spell
by Madame Celeste Honoria

4th

— SPELL INCANTATION —
"Prekarious"

— DESCRIPTION —

This spell keeps stacks of things from falling over, no matter how high. Libraries, government offices, and children's rooms are places where this spell is commonly used.

— SPELL —

Think, "I don't want to clean up a mess," and flick your wand sharply downward, while saying, "Prekarious," out loud.

— COUNTERSPELL —
"Collapsium"

★ Wizard Persona ★

The Head Librarian for 17 years at a government office complex, **Madame Celeste** is credited for creating spells useful to librarians and archivists.

The Coloring Charm
by Koraline Lewis

— SPELL INCANTATION —
"Coltum"

— DESCRIPTION —

This charm makes the victim's skin any color the spell caster wishes.

— SPELL —

Point the wand at the person whose skin color you wish to change and think of a specific color.

— COUNTERSPELL —
"Normalis"

✶ Wizard Persona ✶

Koraline has been creating spells since 1990. Her most popular spells are those used as harmless jokes. She is respected for her high intelligence. She tutors children in magic at a primary school.

A Commanding Spell and Potion
by Dan "Rad" Cliffe

— SPELL INCANTATION —
"Impero homo"

— DESCRIPTION —
This is a spell and potion to make people do as you say.
Potion ingredients:
> Five grams of salt from the Dead Sea
> Ten spoons of honey
> One full ink cartridge (any color)
> A drink the victim likes
> 50 ml. of your sweat

— SPELL —
First make the potion in the following way:
> You need to take a glass,
> Add salt from the sea of dead,
> Add the 50 ml. of sweat,
> And stir with a spoon of lead.

> Take the honey in a bowl,
> Add to it the ink,
> Stir the mixture 'round and 'round,
> Then you're ready to add the drink.

> Thirdly, add the favorite drink.
> The potion will need to wait a year.
> After that the potion is ready,
> And tell the victim to drink a beer.

Wave your wand over the ingredients and say, "Impero homo."
Now they will be yours to command.

✷ Wizard Persona ✷

Dan "Rad" Cliffe is a cool student at the Glamorgan School for Sorcerer's Apprentices.

The Eavesdropping Spell

by Fayla

— SPELL INCANTATION —

"Phlyondewal"

— DESCRIPTION —

This spell creates an eavesdropping device in the shape of a fly, which can attach itself to the wall in a room where you would like to overhear the conversation.

— SPELL —

Make very short vibrating motions with your wand and make a low buzzing sound before and after you recite the spell.

— COUNTERSPELL —

"Phlyswatter"

✷ Wizard Persona ✷

Fayla is a witch best known for combining nutmeg and chili powder with fairy dust to produce Poppers, a highly popular party spell.

The Hand of Fire Spell

by Ravenna C. Tan

— SPELL INCANTATION —

"Palma ignicula"

— DESCRIPTION —

This spell produces a small flame dancing in the palm of your hand. At first glance this spell appears to be only a parlor trick, but it is actually quite useful for lighting candles and campfires or even crusting crème brulée.

Caution: It is best to practice this spell in private, away from flammable objects, books, and papers.

— SPELL —

Speak the incantation, "Palma ignicula," to make a small flame appear over the palm of your hand. If the spell is cast with more force, however, the size and strength of the flame increases.

Once mastered, the subtle flame makes a wonderful first impression. It's also a useful, and dramatic, way to get rid of junk mail.

— COUNTERSPELL —

Close your hand or press your palms together.

✴ Wizard Persona ✴

Ravenna C. Tan studied Advanced Potions and Healing Arts for the last two decades at the Swiss Institute of Pharmacopeia. Her hobby is flame and fire spells.

The "Hare" Hearing Spell

by Mulchik Moodrost

— SPELL INCANTATION —

"Harable"

— DESCRIPTION —

This spell, used on yourself, allows you to hear with the enhanced auditory reception of a rabbit.

— SPELL —

Point the wand over your head, wave it clockwise, and say, "Harable." The spell takes effect immediately.

— COUNTERSPELL —

Point the wand over your head, wave it counterclockwise, and say, "Ex-harable."

✴ Wizard Persona ✴

Mulchik Moodrost specializes in lagomorphic potions for desert rabbits, which help them avoid predators.

The Head Music Spell

by Katie Rodriguez

— SPELL INCANTATION —
"Musicasearas"

— DESCRIPTION —

This spell is used to play a song in your head without having to use an external source (iPod, CD player, radio). You can use it at school, in the car, or when you're playing sports. With this spell, you can take the joy of music with you everywhere.

— SPELL —

Think of the title, artist, lyrics, or tune to any song you want to hear. Say "Musicasearas" and the song will immediately begin playing in your head. You can change the volume up or down by saying "Musicasearas up" (or "down").

— COUNTERSPELL —

To stop the song, say, **"Musicasearas off."**

✶ Wizard Persona ✶

Katie Rodriguez enjoys experimenting with new spells and potions. When she's not using magic, she enjoys listening to music, playing sports, reading, watching television, and spending time with her family and friends. She makes time to study and maintains top marks at school.

The Indestructible Charm

by Augustus Black

— SPELL INCANTATION —
"Impervio destruci"

— DESCRIPTION —

This charm will make any object indestructible.

— SPELL —

Hold your wand at shoulder height and make two counterclock-wise circles, ending with a sharp flick. Point at the object in question and say, "Impervio destruci."

✶ Wizard Persona ✶

The inventor of the Ash Arrow racing broom, **Augustus** owns and operates the "swift witch" racing track in London.

The Inspiration Charm
by Lee Carter

Honorable Mention

— SPELL INCANTATION —
"Renidas Insravis"

— DESCRIPTION —

This charm is used to induce inspiration. For example, if a writer has writer's block, this charm could show him an inspirational object, like a book or a film, that would inspire him. When used, the inspirational object will begin to glow a cerulean hue, which will inspire him further.

— SPELL —

This is a nonverbal spell, but you must "think" the incantation. Hold your wand and twist your wrist counterclockwise, then down, then up, and then clockwise.

— COUNTERSPELL —

If anything goes wrong, say, **"Renidas venavreus."**

✴ Wizard Persona ✴

Lee Carter has been writing since age six. Born in England but currently living in the U.S., she plans on eventually returning to England. She currently writes about undiscovered creatures like the Endruffle.

The Invisibility Spell
by Adreiling

— SPELL INCANTATION —

"Occulto"

— DESCRIPTION —

This spell makes you invisible. It's especially useful if you don't have an invisibility cloak.

— SPELL —

Concentrate on something that frightens you the most, and then say the incantation, "Occulto."

— COUNTERSPELL —

"Declaro"

✴ Wizard Persona ✴

Adreiling studies dragon summoning, yoga, and shape shifting. She is recognized for her talents as a playwright and a breeder of gryphons.

The Magic Detection Spell
by Christine Lee Gengaro

— SPELL INCANTATION —
"Aperio cantio"

— DESCRIPTION —
This spell detects charms and spells that have been placed on non-magical objects. Magical law enforcers can use the spell to insure no one has been illegally charming nonmagical objects.

Enforcers following the movements of dark witches and wizards may use this spell to find clues as to their whereabouts and track them.

— SPELL —
Wave your wand over the object suspected of being charmed and say, "Aperio cantio."

⋆ Wizard Persona ⋆

Christine is a fulltime professor of music at Los Angeles City College. She holds a Ph.D. in Historical Musicology from the University of Southern California. Living among nonmagic folk, Christine strives to show her students the magic of music, reading, and language. She resides in Los Angeles and has recently completed her first novel.

The Mapping Charm
by Olly Umphumfry

— SPELL INCANTATION —

"Slindeferous cartigrous"

— DESCRIPTION —

This spell is used to find a stranded person. It draws a map and highlights in green the area where the stranded person can be found. The person's specific location is marked in red.

— SPELL —

Concentrate on the things around you and say, "Slindeferous cartigrous."

— COUNTERSPELL —

"Lomaticus"

★ Wizard Persona ★

Olly Umphumfry has worked in a bagel factory all of her life. She is best known for her writing skills and lives in Concord, New Hampshire.

The Merperson Spell
by Preussia

— SPELL INCANTATION —
"Merformdia"

— DESCRIPTION —
This spell will turn a female human into a mermaid or a male human into a merman. This spell is great for people who want to learn more about the ocean through firsthand experience.

— SPELL —
Point your wand toward the sky. Think about the ocean, and then think about swimming with fish or other marine creatures. Say, "Merformdia." Flick your wand at the person's legs and the transformation will begin.

— COUNTERSPELL —
"Sapienformdia"

✶ Wizard Persona ✶

Preussia hopes to become a wildlife veterinarian. She has always been interested in legendary creatures, especially mermaids.

The Money-Producing Spell
by Noonie

— SPELL INCANTATION —

"Deniro proliferous"

— DESCRIPTION —

This profitable spell will produce bills or coins in the denominations of your choice from a tree, bush, or flower.

— SPELL —

Point your wand at any tree, bush, or flower and say, "Deniro proliferous."

— NUANCES —

It helps if you think of the form of money (bills or coins) and the denominations/amounts you want.

✶ Wizard Persona ✶

Noonie travels extensively throughout the world using the new-found wealth she realized through the use of this spell.

The Mood-Setting Spell
by Isabelle Imaginere

— SPELL INCANTATION —
"Ambiens decorare"

— DESCRIPTION —

This spell creates a virtual environment by altering the appearance of the décor of any space, indoor or outdoor.

— SPELL —

Use your wand and slowly trace a large circle in the air in front of you, then make a quick flick into its center. Slowly say, "Ambiens," as you draw the circle while imagining in detail how you would like the environment to appear. Then say, "Decorare!" as you flick the wand.

— COUNTERSPELL —
"Effrego"

★ Wizard Persona ★

Isabelle is originally from Paris but currently lives in Hollywood, California. She uses her magical abilities to create environments for theme parks and movie sets.

The Parting Water Spell
by Professor Daiveann Raimunde

— SPELL INCANTATION —
"Manowai mahele kaholo"

— DESCRIPTION —
This spell creates a part in a body of water when you need to cross it and cannot find an alternate route.

— SPELL —
Point your wand at the body of water and imagine it parting.

⋆ Wizard Persona ⋆

Professor Raimunde, who teaches Theatrical Arts in Northern Ireland, is best known for her incorporation of magical creatures in the technical aspects of stage design.

The Party Popper Spell
by Cookie Minwaggle

— SPELL INCANTATION —
"Tiro carta"

— DESCRIPTION —
This spell produces colorful confetti out from your wand tip. It's especially useful at parties and special occasions.

— SPELL —
Point your wand in the direction that you want to spread the confetti, say, "Tiro carta," and spread your arms wide.

— COUNTERSPELL —
Use any stopping spell.

✦ Wizard Persona ✦

Cookie is the only witch in her family, though her Aunt Helen is reputed to show magical tendencies. Because her parents did not want her to attend a wizardry school, she was not able to attend until she turned 18. After moving to England to develop her magical abilities at a wizardry school, she created the Party Popper Spell. She currently owns a bakery at a famous wizard shopping alley.

The Quieting Spell
by Deandra

— SPELL INCANTATION —
"Quietrahhfon"

— DESCRIPTION —
This spell will make any noisy object lower its volume or, if necessary, render it mute.

— SPELL —
Concentrate on the noise that you want lowered. Point your wand and flick it three times at the noisy object.

The Rehearsal Spell

by Rolith the Great of the late Eerox Dynasty

— SPELL INCANTATION —

"Phantomorum"

— DESCRIPTION —

Wouldn't it be great if you could rehearse the important events in your life beforehand, so you can put your best foot forward? With this spell, you can! Rehearse how to ask a girl out on a date, how to negotiate with your boss for a raise, or how to tell your significant other that things between you two have run their course. Just conjure up a phantom replica of the person you need to talk to, and then rehearse your conversations as often as you'd like, until you get it letter-perfect.

Try various scenarios. Make sure it's perfect before you actually have the conversation with the real person.

— SPELL —

Picture in your mind the person with whom you'd like to have the conversation. Then flick the wand quickly side-to-side six times while reciting the incantation.

✷ Wizard Persona ✷

Rolith the Great is a hermit who resides in a collapsed underground bunker from World War II.

The Revealing Spell

by Erika Najera

— SPELL INCANTATION —

"Avioshin"

— DESCRIPTION —

This spell helps reveal hidden spirits or people. It's very useful if you want to find a ghost, spirit, or poltergeist, or someone using an invisibility cloak.

— SPELL —

Concentrate hard on the person or spirit you want to render visible, point your wand in the general direction, and say, "Avioshin."

— COUNTERSPELL —

"Aviosno"

★ Wizard Persona ★

Erika Najera has maintained a phoenix society since 1993. She donates phoenix feathers to the Phoenix Wands company for wand construction. She lives on a phoenix farm near a forest.

The Revelation Spell

by Hypatia Hapsburg

— SPELL INCANTATION —
"Recludo"

— DESCRIPTION —

This spell is primarily useful during exams. It reveals facts you studied but just can't quite recall by bringing information back to the surface.

Caution: If used too frequently, this spell can cause short-term memory loss.

— SPELL —

Concentrate hard on the fact you wish to recall and then say or think, "Recludo."

— NUANCES —

This spell works best for facts and dates.

— COUNTERSPELL —
"Recognosco"

⋆ Wizard Persona ⋆

Hypatia was raised by a family of apothecaries and gardeners, whose roots in the U.S. go back to 1900. An educator who has created many useful spells to help students excel, Hypatia is known for her work in cataloging herbal ingredients used in potion making.

The See-Through Spell

by Cameron Erskine

— SPELL INCANTATION —

"Spectrolious"

— DESCRIPTION —

This spell will allow you to see through walls or doors. It's especially useful when there's an enemy outside your door because it gives you time to prepare for the attack or get away.

— SPELL —

Point your wand to your eyes, and then say, "Spectrolious," and focus on the wall or door you wish to see through.

— COUNTERSPELL —

"Suoilorteeps"

⋆ Wizard Persona ⋆

Cameron Erskine makes magical candy boxes.

Self-Performing Instrument Spell

by Ginger Potronus

— SPELL INCANTATION —

"Lascivio unus instrument"

— DESCRIPTION —

This spell makes an instrument play itself. It may be used when you need to distract someone or when you want to listen to music while doing something else.

— SPELL —

Concentrate on a song and the instrument. Then say, "Lascivio unus instrument," move your wand clockwise, and flick your wrist. The instrument should then start playing. (If it doesn't, you haven't concentrated enough.)

⋆ Wizard Persona ⋆

Ginger has played in many symphonies and has won many awards for her performances. She is currently studying American music styles and playing recitals with the clarinet, trumpet, and flute.

The Spell to Create Art
by Arika

— SPELL INCANTATION —
"Doco color"

— DESCRIPTION —

This spells lets you use your wand to draw or paint. It can be used with any color. The color streams out of the wand. You guide the wand as you would a paintbrush, crayon, or pencil.

— SPELL —

1. Find the color you want and touch it with the tip of your wand, say the spell, and begin painting.
2. If the color you need is not within reach, say the color before you do the spell. (This method is slower because your wand needs to make the color on its own.)

★ Wizard Persona ★

Arika is a young witch with extraordinary talent. She excels at most subjects in school and has been known to make up her own spells. She is an only child and her parents are Maglinots.

A Spell to Create a Sense of Wonder

by Professor Vox Venificus

— SPELL INCANTATION —

"Instill admiratio"

— DESCRIPTION —

The older people get, the less likely they are to respond to the wonders of the world, the endlessly fascinating and curious world that children live in daily. Especially useful for aging baby boomers, this powerful spell instills a sense of wonder when looking at a man-made work of art or the work of nature.

— SPELL —

Point your wand and flick once at the person whom you want to enchant with a sense of wonder. The spell does wear off, though, so repeated castings are necessary.

✳ Wizard Persona ✳

Professor Vox Venificus is a word scribe who lives in the enchanted village of Colonial Williamsburg in Virginia.

The Spell to Identify Liars

by Katriona McCallum

— SPELL INCANTATION —

"Mentiroso identificus"

— DESCRIPTION —

This spell allows the caster to know if the person speaking to him is lying by creating a red vapor, visible only to the performer of the spell, to issue from the speaker's mouth with each lie. This spell is very handy when students are giving excuses about unfinished homework.

— SPELL —

This is a very difficult spell. Say, "Mentiroso indentificus," and tap the air twice with the wand, then flick once, and tap again.

★ Wizard Persona ★

For twenty years, **Ms. McCallum** has been a history of magical arts instructor at the Saleritus School of Magic, which is located on an invisible island in the middle of the Great Salt Lake.

The Spell to Repair Anything

by Quentarius Cabolt

— SPELL INCANTATION —

"Teraundae assula"

— DESCRIPTION —

This spell can fix a broken magical object.

— SPELL —

Concentrate on the object you wish to fix, and then wave your wand around it in a circular motion.

✶ Wizard Persona ✶

Quentarius Cabolt is well known for his healing spells. He is most famous, however, for his discovery that griffin saliva is potent and can be used as an energy booster.

The Surefooted Spell

by Madam Mallory

— SPELL INCANTATION —

"May every step I take be right.
May all of my misfortune be left behind."

— DESCRIPTION —

This spell insures that the spell caster will not stray from his intended life path and will continue toward his destiny with minimum malady.

This spell can be very useful when contemplating a life change or at any point of transition—a new career, school graduation, or deciding upon a permanent appearance-altering charm.

— SPELL —

1. In the evening, take two straight pins and place them on each side of your interior windowsill. To the one on the right side, move your wand over it in a clockwise motion and repeat three times, "May every step I take be right." Cover the pin with a square of cloth.
2. To the pin on the left side, move your wand over it in a counterclockwise motion and repeat three times, "May all of my misfortune be left behind." Cover the pin with a square of cloth.
3. Leave the pins on your windowsill overnight. In the morning, pierce them through the respective soles of your shoes (left pin, left shoe; right pin, right shoe). If you can leave the pins in without causing foot injury, the spell will work more powerfully.
4. Repeat the spell each night before intended use and enjoy confident and catastrophe-free days.

✴ Wizard Persona ✴

After being named **Mallory** (or "ill-omened one") by her Maglinot parents, she tasked herself at a very young age to develop lucky charms and good fortune-inducing potions that would work even on the unluckiest witches and wizards.

While Mallory still has not been able to produce anything strong enough to work on herself, her spells do the trick for the rest of us.

The Tail Sprouting Spell
by Heather

— SPELL INCANTATION —
"Caudatus"

— DESCRIPTION —
This spell will cause the victim to sprout a tail. It is used mostly as a practical joke, but is also useful when someone—particularly a sibling—annoys you.

— SPELL —
Concentrate on the type of animal or reptile tail you wish to attach to the victim, flick your wand down, and say, "Caudatus."

— COUNTERSPELL —
Flick your wand up and say, **"Defluo."**

✷ Wizard Persona ✷

Heather has been breeding phoenixes at her home since 2000. She often uses wandless magic.

The Undoing Spell
by Sanjilla Ozga

— SPELL INCANTATION —

"Take back the spell and make it all well."

— DESCRIPTION —

This spell is used when a spell caster experiences remorse and wishes to undo his last spell. This is most often used on minor spells—binding, levitating, dismantling—and cannot be used on life-altering spells.

— SPELL —

With your wand in hand, twirl your wand clockwise and say, "Take back the spell and make it all well."

✴ Wizard Persona ✴

Sanjilla has maintained a witch's greenhouse for centuries. She was recently voted as the favored ingredient supplier to the Chief Witch of Legionton.

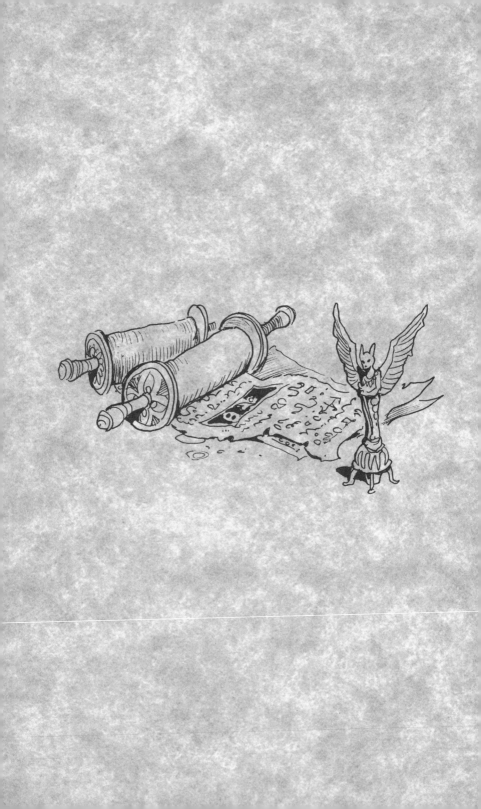

Whimsic Alley
SPELLS

This section has spells from Sir Geoffrey Whimsic, who founded Whimsic Alley in the year 1367. Though Whimsic Alley is his claim to fame, few people realize that he is also credited with the origination of more than six hundred spells, potions, hexes, and charms. He is indisputably one of the more influential wizards of all time. Sir Geoffrey authored fourteen books on spells and potions—most notably *Could You Spell That for Me?*, *Spelling Counts*, and *I Can't Spell to Save My Life*. Many of his books are the definitive texts on spell casting, required reading at most major wizarding academies.

Though generally described as extremely likable, Sir Geoffrey seems to have had few friends. This is due likely to his reputation as a drunkard and a cad. He has often been referred to as a genius, but just as frequently as a raving lunatic. A statue had been erected of him in Brussels, Belgium, commemorating his many advancements in the art of magic. However, one of his detractors, of which there were many, placed a curse on the statue so that it would forever attract the droppings of any birds within a hundred meter radius. The statue is now so covered in bird droppings that it is impossible to distinguish its original shape.

It is rather ironic that Sir Geoffrey, someone often considered one of the principal authorities on spell casting, met his untimely end in a wizard duel with his business partner, who was not known as a particularly adept spell caster. Apparently his opponent was able to master just one significant spell for the duel—a mirroring spell. In the duel, one of Sir Geoffrey's own spells—a highly unusual transformation spell to which only he knew the counterspell—was bounced back at him. No one was ever able to reverse its effects. Sir Geoffrey had been transformed into a tree sloth and lived out his remaining years hanging from a large sycamore tree.

The Blind Love Charm

"Sensiorum"

— DESCRIPTION —

Some say that love is blind. Others call love a temporary state of insanity. But what is clear is that a person in love is oblivious to the faults of the object of his affection, though his friends can see the relationship in a more objective light.

The sensiorum charm is used to help a person see more clearly, to see the object of affection in the same way as others.

— NUANCES —

This challenging spell must be cast by at least three wizards in unison.

Caution: Once the charm has taken effect, the formerly clueless, now enlightened, person may become violent. He may express extreme anger toward the former object of his affection or directly against himself for being so stupid in the first place.

— COUNTERSPELL —

None. This is an irreversible charm and, as such, should be used with great caution. Not even magic will restore the relationship to its former state of infatuation.

The Appreciation Charm

— SPELL INCANTATION —

"Appreciatus"

— DESCRIPTION —

This charm can be used on a work of art, a written piece, an object of construction, a photo, or a project. Anyone who sees or reads the charmed item will be delighted by it.

Note: While this charm cannot be used on a person, it can be used on a photo or movie of a person.

— SPELL —

Swish and flick once over the item in question and say, "Appreciatus."

— COUNTERSPELL —

Swish and flick once over the item in question and say, **"Despisiatum."**

The Smokestack Spell

"Chimniata"

— DESCRIPTION —

This spell eliminates secondhand smoke and its associated odor by building an invisible chimney around the smoker.

Smoke normally spreads horizontally and then vertically, but when this spell is applied, the smoke will *only* rise (i.e., spread vertically).

— SPELL —

Concentrate on smoke rising. Flick your wand in a slight upward motion.

The Spell to Bring Literary Characters to Life

— SPELL INCANTATION —

"Extracto literum"

— DESCRIPTION —

This spell draws characters out of books and into the real world. Some wizards have wreaked havoc with this spell by extracting notoriously evil characters or monsters from works of literature. Luckily, the counterspell is simple and effective.

— SPELL —

The spell caster must wrap his mind around the character he wishes to extract, recite the spell, "Extracto literum," and make a pulling motion with his wand.

— COUNTERSPELL —

Point the wand and say, "Refictionatum."

The Spell to Remove Calories

— SPELL INCANTATION —
"Nonfatello"

— DESCRIPTION —

This spell removes all calories from a plate of food without affecting its taste or texture.

— SPELL —

Point your wand at the plate of food and say, "Nonfatello."

The Mute Hex

"Silencia"

— DESCRIPTION —

This is a dueling spell that was originally intended to silence an opponent so an incantation, curse, or hex could not be uttered. However, it also has proven effective when used in noncombat situations: crying babies, whining children, and barking dogs.

Note: This verbal spell was created before the invention of the nonverbal, or thought, spell. A mute opponent who is sufficiently skilled can still respond and attack with the nonverbal spells, hexes, jinxes, or curses.

— SPELL —

Wiggle your ears and stare intently at the intended subject. If you cannot wiggle your ears, whisper, "Silencia."

The Space Compression Spell

— SPELL INCANTATION —

"Compreesium"

— DESCRIPTION —

This simple and practical spell creates a temporary space of up to approximately forty meters by compressing nearby objects. The result: It creates space where none previously existed.

This is most often used for creating a parking space, stadium or concert seats, or a camping/picnic space. It's also used to create more space for newcomers at a crowded table. Obviously, it can be used to cut into long lines, but that practice is generally frowned upon.

— SPELL —

Picture the size of the space required and flick your wand quickly, left and right.

— COUNTERSPELL —

"Compreesium restora" (Use this when the space is no longer needed, to put things back to normal.)

The Word Balloon Spell

"Comic balloonus"

— DESCRIPTION —

This simple spell reveals the inner thoughts of a person by creating a word balloon (as seen in a comic book) over his head. It can also work on animals.

— SPELL —

Make three circles of increasing size with your wand and aim it at the subject.

— COUNTERSPELL —

Most trained wizards are taught at an early age to use the **"Thoughtius blocutia"** incantation on themselves to prevent the inadvertent revelation of one's inner thoughts.

The Emotion Charm

"Izofunuther"

— DESCRIPTION —

This spell enables the target of the spell to feel the emotions of another person. It can be used to show a man how a woman feels or vice versa. This charm is often used by wizard therapists on their patients.

Caution: Some males who feel the emotions of women have experienced uncontrollable weeping for long periods of time.

— SPELL —

Concentrate on extracting the essence of the target's soul into your wand and say the incantation, "Izofunuther."

— COUNTERSPELL —

Unfortunately, it does not exist, though patients have frequently requested one.

Wizard Wears, Wares, and Where?

BY STAN GOLDIN

Wizard Wear: Assembling a Wizarding Wardrobe

While most of us prefer that Maglinots not be able to identify us as members of the Magique community, our mode of dress often gives us away. Pictures of wizards throughout the centuries show distinctive dressing behavior, which instantly identifies them as such, even to the untrained eye.

The Wizard Hat

The most distinctive article of wizard apparel, the wizard hat, ironically came about by happenstance. The earliest wizards wore something akin to a turban, owing to their Arabic and Oriental roots. In 1141, a diminutive Finnish wizard with legendary powers, named Vhenschnopple, was a member of the court of King Llewellyn, who relied heavily on Vhenschnopple's powers of sorcery. Llewellyn demanded that he always be able to spot his sorcerer, even in a crowd. Because Vhenschnopple was so short, the king made him wear a special, tall, pointed hat so that he could be located easily when the king needed him.

The tall, pointed wizard hat came to symbolize the position of Sorcerer to the Court. Subsequent appointees—even those who were tall and lanky—all wore the wizard hat, later adorned with jewels or sparkles depicting moons and stars. The tall hat, which became officially designated as the uniform of the Court Wizard, eventually caught on as the fashion among everyday wizards.

It should be noted that nearly every wizard owns a hat, whether or not he chooses to wear it. Until recently, there had been little variation in the wizard hat over the centuries. In fact, current fashion still incorporates the traditional hat for most occasions. Stars and moons are still the most common adornment.

Trendy designers, however, have begun experimenting with alternative materials and fashions to add variety and spice to this wardrobe staple, so that the wizard hat has become more individualistic. It's not unusual for today's wizard to own two or more hats to express different moods or to be worn for different functions.

Most important is the formal hat, to be worn at important functions, ceremonies, and official occasions. This hat is nearly always tall and pointy, although wizards from other cultures may wear formal hats indigenous to their culture.

The informal hat is worn for various outings—during journeys, casual visits to town, and under routine occupational pursuits. The pointed wizard hat is rarely worn on such occasions. In fact, polite society has finally accepted the flaccid point which had previously only been worn by more bohemian wizards. Adventurous wizards have begun exploring the very early roots of hat style with the turban and the fez when informal hat wear is appropriate.

The casual hat is typically worn only at the most casual times—at indoor social events or while lounging.

I recommend shopping only at reputable Wizard Haberdasheries for your wizard hat. Although they are widely available elsewhere, nonreputable sources will have no sense of current fashion, and you may end up looking like a buffoon in a hat that Maglinots somehow think looks like a wizard hat.

The Robe, Cape, and Cloak

Many people, even among the Magiques, often confuse robes, capes, and cloaks. The basic difference between these three garments, though there are other differences as well, is that robes have sleeves, cloaks often provide armholes, and capes have neither. Each type of garment may or may not have a hood. Each is appropriate wizard wear, but only the robe is acceptable in formal situations. Therefore, I will focus on just the robe, noting that a functional cloak or cape will suffice in informal situations.

While the wizard hat, discussed earlier, is basically an adornment, the wizard robe is an essential garment. The robe predates the wizard hat by about six centuries. It was originally made with long, billowy sleeves capable of hiding rudimentary diversions. The billowy sleeves have remained a part of the garment, even though the trickery has been almost entirely replaced by real magic.

The functionality of the robe is in its hidden (or charmed) pockets. Pockets are normally charmed to appear invisible, regardless of how bulky their contents may be. An experienced wizard carries many things in his robe lining pockets. First and foremost is his wand—for many, their most powerful tool. Wizards adept in the use of alchemy may carry many of their more common potion supplies in their pockets. Others have been known to carry orbs, crystal balls, and even magical creatures in their robe pockets. Wizards are often reluctant to say how many pockets they have in their robes, and I

suspect many don't even know. One wizard, Arloftian, was reputed to have had upwards of 2,700 pockets in his robe. It was mused that he was always able to instantly find exactly what he needed, except for a coin when it came time to paying a check.

There are robes for all occasions. Formal robes, often called dress robes, can look like a formal tuxedo or have all the pomp and circumstance of the Victorian era. There are also work robes, ceremonial robes, school robes, and casual robes. Dress robes, ceremonial robes, and casual robes do not have the functionality of work robes and school robes.

Fashion designers have taken great liberties with robes over the years. Other than uniform robes, such as those worn by school students, no two robes look exactly alike. It is said that a robe takes on the personality of its wearer. As a result, most wizards are reluctant to ever part with a robe, no matter how frayed and tattered it becomes. Most wizards are capable of performing simple spells to remedy wear and tear. Some flamboyant wizards may wear a different robe every day. Some even refuse to wear the same robe twice.

You may be able to find bargain robes at places such as Wizards Warehouse or even at Seers. Such bargain robes tend to lack true functionality. Therefore, discriminating wizards will shop at a specialty store, such as Habber and Dasher, located on Whimsic Alley. Habber and Dasher has been suiting wizards for several centuries now. It was reported that at one point, every member of the Supreme Council of Magiques was wearing a Habber and Dasher creation.

Student Uniforms

All accredited wizardry schools throughout the world require students to wear a uniform. While there may be slight variations from school to school, the student uniform generally includes a school robe, a sweater, and a tie. For schools in colder climates, a scarf is often recommended. Capes and cloaks are often permitted. Robes are suggested to be fully functional, and have many invisible charmed pockets. The one essential pocket is the wand pocket. Some schools require that robes be standardized—all the same—while other schools permit certain freedoms, such as linings in house colors. Such schools also frequently allow that ties and sweaters be in house colors rather than school colors. Consult your school or academy for specific wardrobe requirements.

~~ 2 ~~

Creating a Bewitching Wardrobe

To the witch or future witch reading this chapter, you've come a long way, baby. Until very recently, the witch's wardrobe was, at best, mundane. Most current day designers call the "traditional" witch garb hideously atrocious. Tall, black, pointed hat (derivative of the pointed wizard's hat, but with a wide brim), black button-down long flowing dress, orange and black striped knee socks, and black shoes with a curled up point. Other than the knee socks, which some witches consider retro chic, there isn't a witch alive today who would be caught dead in such an outfit.

Witch's Wear Daily conducts a semiannual trade show called Magic. The following are the latest trends identified at the most recent Magic trade show:

Hats: The tall, pointed witch's hat has never really disappeared. But it has evolved into something entirely different. Designers have added texture to the hat with materials such as suede, faux fur, and leather. Adornments such as colorful ribbons, feathers, and crepe help to make each hat unique. Today's witch has a plethora of choices when it comes to hats.

Robes: The traditional high-collared, flowing black dress was long ago replaced by the sophisticated robe. Heavily influenced by its male counterpart, the robe has become the most essential piece of the witch's wardrobe. Equipped, like the wizard robe, with dozens or hundreds of secret invisible pockets, the witch's robe has become highly functional without sacrificing fashion. Most fashion-conscious witches have more than a dozen robes for every occasion, although unlike wizards, the ladies commonly dress in nonmagical garb during elegant occasions. Still, the robe, owing to both its visual appeal and its functionality, is the main staple of every witch's wardrobe.

Knee socks are still a favorite among younger witches, who also favor short skirts, shorts, and jeans just as their Maglinot counterparts do. Grown witches tend to be more staid in their appearance, but still have a keen eye toward fashion.

Students are required to wear uniform robes in either the school colors, or in some cases, the specific house colors. Uniforms also require matching colored ties, sweaters, scarves, white oxford style shirts, and a uniform skirt (commonly in gray, khaki, or navy).

Shopping for Witch's Wear

While many witch garments are available at discount chain stores such as Seers, Magic Outfitters, and WitchMart, most discriminating witches will shop at a specialty store such as Habber and Dasher, which is located on Whimsic Alley. Unlike the chain stores, Habber and Dasher understands how to combine fashion with functionality to create a truly magical effect.

Wizard Wares: Wands

Selecting the right wand can be like
selecting the right kitten. Any of
them may be okay but only one will
be the perfect companion for you.

The Ascention Collection
features wands for
beginners—at the beginner
price of just under $8.

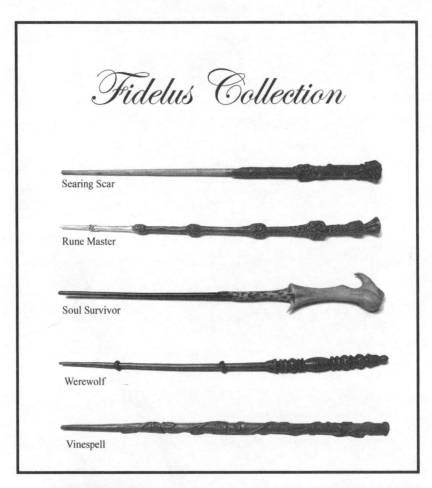

Fidelus Collection

Searing Scar

Rune Master

Soul Survivor

Werewolf

Vinespell

Sophisticated wizards gravitate toward the Fidelus and Lumos Collections from Phoenix Wands. Each wand comes in a velvet-lined wand box and is priced at just under $24.

The Lumos Collection

The Athena

The Protector

The Guardian

The Dragon

The Scourge

The Achiever

The Sage

The Holly

At the core of The Searing Scar wand is a phoenix feather. Compatible traits for wizards considering this wand include boldness, loyalty, and impetuousness. Measures 15 inches.

Compatible traits for wizards considering The Werewolf wand include creativity, loyalty, and intuition. Measures 15 inches.

The Serpent's Heir wand contains a phoenix feather at its core. Wizards considering this wand will typically exhibit such traits as cunning, brilliance, and pride. Measures 15 inches.

The first shop on your right after you enter Whimsic Alley is Habber & Dasher, clothiers to wizards for hundreds of years. The shop features the finest in robes and cloaks, sweaters, ties, and scarves.

Phoenix Wands offers more than thirty styles of magic wands. This quaint shop allows wizards to test their wands until just the right fit is attained.

Widdleshaft's Quill and Ink shop features exotic feather quills, dozens of writing and drawing journals, seals and sealing wax, and a plethora of romance-era writing instruments, ink wells, and more.

It has been said that all the knowledge that a wizard must possess is contained in the volumes located in the Whimsic Book Shop. Specialty books cover subjects such as spells, potions, divination, tarot, magical customs, magical creatures, and more.

To your left upon entering Whimsic Alley is the world-famous Phoenix Wands shop. Phoenix has been making high quality wands since 426 B.C. Its wands have been used by some of the world's most famous witches and wizards.

The entrance to HP Wizard Store, near the rear of Whimsic Alley, never fails to bring a smile to the face of a visitor. The store boasts the world's largest selection of Harry Potter-brand merchandise—all in one place.

Extracted Chapters

from the

WHIMSIC ALLEY
BOOK OF KNOWLEDGE

BY STAN GOLDIN

~ **5** ~

Where Do Wands Come From?

Wands are made from woods of every type. Each wood has its own magical properties. The world's finest wands, however, are said to come from one of only four magical forests on the planet. These forests are all in very remote and highly secret locations. As a boy, I had the opportunity to visit one of these—the Bleeding Forest—since my grandfather was an old school friend of the owner of that forest. I have no idea where the forest is and I suspect neither did my grandfather, as we traveled there by magical means provided by our host.

I'll come back to my experience in the Bleeding Forest, but first let's discuss the other three forests. The most well known is probably the Purple Rain Forest. The best guess is that it is located somewhere in the Amazon in South America. That forest has been producing wands for nearly six hundred years. Visitors have reported that the rain that falls there really is purple. The rain is said to have very dark, magical powers. Practitioners in the dark arts select wands from this forest. A drawback of such wands is that they dry out and must be re-saturated by soaking them in purple rain water for two weeks each year.

The Petrified Forest, though not as well known as the Purple Rain Forest, produces nearly two-thirds of all wands used today. This is due to several factors, not the least of which is the accessibility of the forest. It is said to be located somewhere in Siberia, and it is about three times the size of the other three forests combined. Its woods possess all the magical capabilities as those produced in the more elite forests, but many say they lack the finesse and intuitive properties of the others.

Reputed to be located somewhere in the Australian Outback, the Forest of Dreams (widely referred to as the Dream Forest) produces highly irregular woods that are often unpredictable and difficult to manage. Because of this, only the most experienced and capable witches and wizards would even consider owning a wand from this region. Those who have learned to control the magic in such wands are said to be among the strongest magic practitioners alive.

I said I would tell about my time in the Bleeding Forest. First, let me tell you that the Bleeding Forest is the only magical forest that is entirely owned by a single family, and knowledge of its location is highly guarded. There are several rumors as to its general location. Most believable among these possible locations are the Canadian Rockies, the Bavarian Alps, or the Himalayas. As I said, we were transported there by our hosts, who employed a form of magical transportation I had not experienced before or since. The trees in the forest really did appear to be bleeding. A red, magical sap dripped to the forest floor where it pooled up, saturated the fallen leaves, and penetrated the earth to provide continual nourishment for the trees. The light filtering in from above had a reddish glow, probably because of the sap. It is said that the sap is so powerful that walking on it adds one day to your life for each step you take. Presumably those are healthy days in the middle of your life and not additional sick days added on to the end of your life. I will never forget the feeling I had standing in the middle of the Bleeding Forest. It was as though all magic in the world was emanating from within me. It felt like every finger on my two hands was a powerful wand and that every vein and capillary in my body was a conduit of magical spirits.

Wands produced from the eternal trees in the Bleeding Forest are among the most elite and sought after. The family that owns the forest has been making wands under the Phoenix Wands name for dozens of centuries. Phoenix Wands shop is located on Whimsic Alley, 2717½ Wilshire Boulevard, Santa Monica, California 90403, or on the Wizards and Witches Web at www.whimsicalley.com.

～❀ 6 ❀～

Mastering a Spell

There are thousands of spells. Many spells are nearly identical to other spells, with only very slight differences. In some cases, virtually identical spells may be performed very differently and under very different circumstances with very different outcomes. It would be extremely difficult, even for the most sage of wizards, to memorize all spells—and nearly impossible to master them all.

Before employing a spell, the spell caster must very quickly assess the situation, determine a desired result, and select the proper spell to achieve that result. Sometimes one must make those assessments, determinations, and selections in a few moments time. In the case of a duel, one may have only a split second to react. Simply knowing a spell, even having previously used it, is a far cry from being proficient in its use. It is widely believed that one cannot become proficient with a spell until he or she has employed it at least one hundred times. In her book *Perfect Spelling*, Rionetha Lestumstra identifies ten essential steps to becoming proficient in the use of a spell.

Most accredited wizarding academies teach the first seven steps of spell casting in the primary grades (years). For the most part, the processes involved are rote memorization, basic understanding, and frequent repetition. These seven steps are considered analogous to developing one's vocabulary by learning a word, learning its meaning(s) within various contexts, and using it frequently in speaking or writing until it becomes a natural part of one's vocabulary. As students graduate to secondary school, they begin with the same spells they covered in their early years, but then begin applying steps 8–10 to the learning process. Step 8, the first of the secondary steps, is considered so fundamental that many schools offer classes and/or major tracts based solely on step 8.

1. **Learn to properly pronounce the incantation:** Many spells sound quite similar. The very first thing you must learn about a spell is its exact pronunciation. This includes voice inflexion, compensation for accents, and articulation. Until it can be said precisely and identically each time, the spell has not been mastered.

2. **Memorize the incantation:** Often, teachers tell their students that they must learn to say a spell in their sleep. This is an exaggeration, but the intent is that the spell becomes instinctive. Just as we can formulate instinctive and instantaneous responses when we hear such terms as "over," "red light," and "marco," we should be able to do the same with a given spell.

3. Learn the methods and nuances of casting the spell: Casting a spell generally entails more than just pointing a wand and saying some words. There are nuances—thoughts, motions, and emotions—that the caster must make and have in order to properly execute a spell. Learning a spell means learning how to generate these nuances and coordinate them with the incantation. Mastering the spell involves making these nuances as instinctual as the incantation. Can you instantly and instinctively turn on an emotion of blissful happiness when you're under extreme pressure or threatening circumstances? You'd better be able to if you expect to master a spell that requires such nuances.

4. Understand the effects of the spell: When we first learn a spell, we have certain preconceived notions about its effects. When we truly study it, we may find that the effects are somewhat different from what's anticipated. Take, for example, a simple spell such as one that boils water. Very straightforward, we think at first. Yet, how much do we really know without learning about it and experimenting with it? How large a pot can we boil? A quart? A gallon? How about a whole swimming pool? Knowing what the spell is capable of doing helps us know when to use it and when not to attempt it. That knowledge only comes with a lot of study and practice.

5. Be aware of any side effects of the spell: A commonly used spell that changes the color of a garment has the side effect of making that garment reek after twenty-seven hours. This is a simple side effect of a simple spell. Imagine the complex side effects of complex spells, such as those cast upon a person or animal. It's important to know them before attempting the spell. A harmless spell one might cast on young people may have a very detrimental effect on older people.

6. **Know the counterspell (if any):** Many spells have counterspells that either block or reverse the effects of the spell. Knowing the counterspell and having it fresh in your mind is key to developing a proficiency with the spell.

7. **Know how to reverse the effects of the spell:** Not all spells have counterspells. And counterspells, when they do exist, may not fully reverse the effects of using the spell in the first place. Finally, since different spells may have the same perceived effect, you may not be privy to which spell was actually used and may have to deal with the effect rather than with a specific counterspell.

8. **Determine when the spell should be used:** During the final seconds of a close basketball game, the coach will generally call a time-out to set up the last play or defense. He knows his players will have very little time to think and he wants to cover every possible scenario with them so they know precisely what they should do, depending on the actions of the other team. In real life, we don't have the luxury of calling a time-out. We must think on our feet and employ the proper spell, and then perform it correctly. Therefore, it is vital that we have preplanned the conditions under which we should employ a particular spell. It often takes months or years to contemplate all the situations where a spell might be employed. One person's list will very likely differ from another's. Therefore, it's a difficult subject to teach—sort of like creative writing.

9. **Know when *not* to use the spell:** Just as there are opportune times to use a particular spell, there are generally certain situations in which you definitely would not want to use it. Someone who excels at the card game Blackjack sets personal rules for himself— don't split a pair of tens or don't double down if the dealer is showing a ten. A spell caster, too, should pre-establish a set of rules about when *not* to use a particular spell. For example, one would not use the smokestack spell while there are gremlins present— the results could be catastrophic. Some spells, while legal, are not socially acceptable in certain situations. The spell caster must be aware of those. In dueling, you should be aware of a spell's limitations and not use it if it can be easily countered or if it is ineffectual.

10. Know what to do if the spell is being used on you: When students begin learning step 10, they tend to assume it refers to defending oneself in a duel. While this is certainly one of the situations in which a familiarity with step 10 is critical, it is hardly the only one. In fact, when dueling, the only way to fully defend oneself against a particular spell is to anticipate its use and block it before it can take effect. However, what if you are the object of a love spell or a silencing spell? In order to deal with such situations, you must have a broad familiarity with spells in general so that you can assess which spell you are under and determine how to deal with it.

With so much to learn and practice in order to become proficient with a spell, it's easy to see why most wizards tend to focus on a manageable number—usually somewhere between 100 and 150—and use those under the vast majority of circumstances. Seven years at any accredited wizarding academy should develop proficiency with about 50 to 70 basic spells. One can often gain an advantage over other wizards by learning which spells they tend to favor, so you would be wise to not let others see you using the same spells over and over again.

A recent development in how to learn spells is through virtual reality games, such as World of Spellcraft, which requires players to use many spells on short notice in simulated situations.

7

Spells, Charms, Hexes, Curses, and Jinxes

The Magique—the community of magical beings—uses the term "spells" to encompass many forms of magical actions. These include charms, hexes, curses, jinxes, and spells. In this book, we have followed this convention of including all of these forms of magic under the all-encompassing term "spells."

It is almost more relevant to specify what is *not* meant by the use of the term "spells" than what is. When referring to "spells," we are *not* including any form of magic that requires ingredients common to the practice of voodoo, such as blood, hairs, skin shavings, saliva, or personal possessions of some person or thing.

Brewster's Dictionary of Magical Terms defines the word spell as "a term used to describe a wide variety of charms, hexes, curses and jinxes." Yet there are subtle differences between these various forms of spells. The book *Spelling for the Reasonably Well Informed* identifies them as follows:

Spells: Spells may be good or bad. They are highly specific and generally take the form of action/reaction. A spell can be any magical action that causes a reaction that would not be likely to occur under nonmagical circumstances. **Example:** A man casts a spell on his wife that causes her lips to become very thick and sensual.

Charms: A charm is a form of magic that generally has a beneficial effect on the object of the charm. Charms performed on objects usually make those objects appear, in one way or another, more desirable than they were before. Charms performed on people or animals may result in improved traits or characteristics. A person affected by a charm may have increased confidence, better luck, or an improved appearance. **Example:** A father places a charm on his daughter to make her irresistible to any man with substantial wealth.

Hexes: Hexes are far less common than they once were. A hex is used to make a person, animal, or object unlucky. However, the results are unpredictable. In placing a hex on something or someone, you have no control over the type of bad luck that will befall them. For this reason, most wizards today tend to favor the more specific curses and jinxes. **Example:** Someone places a hex on a diamond ring, bestowing upon its owner perpetual bad luck.

Curses: Like a hex, a curse causes some evil or misfortune to fall upon its victim. Unlike a hex, though, curses are very specific. The particular curse used defines precisely the misfortune that will befall its victim and under what circumstances. Because of the amount of control it affords, the curse has become far more popular today than the hex. **Example:** Someone casts a curse on his enemy, causing warts to spring out on his face.

Jinxes: A jinx can be applied to a person or an object. It bestows a specific misfortune upon anyone who performs a certain action related to that person or object. It is not as direct as a curse, but its effect can be every bit as specific. **Example:** Someone casts a jinx on his enemy's daughter so that anyone who marries her will die penniless within one year.

Acknowledgments

We wish to thank all the fine folks at Hampton Roads Publishing, especially Bob and Jack, who had faith in this book; the book's editor, Tania Seymour, who is surely one of Harry Potter's most ardent fans; and Jane Hagaman, who shepherded this book through production.

We owe special thanks to Tim Kirk, whose whimsical touch was exactly what we were looking for in terms of the cover and frontispiece.

We also would like to thank Mischa McCortney and Hans Christianson for modeling Whimsic Alley clothing. Likewise, we'd like to thank Britton McDaniel and Jacob Edwards for posing as wizards for photos taken on the campus of William and Mary, to the bemused look of students and tourists in Colonial Williamsburg.

We'd like to thank every person who took the time to submit a spell, and especially thank those who submitted more than one. Congratulations, of course, are in order for those whose spells we selected for inclusion, for you have thereby earned eternal fame and glory, and our undying thanks, as well.

Note: George Beahm here. I'd like to thank my long-suffering wife, Mary, who as always had numerous suggestions that improved the book and served as my sounding board on this project.

About the Editors and Artist

George Beahm is the author of several fantasy-related books, including *The J. R. R. Tolkien Sourcebook*; *Muggles and Magic: An Unofficial Guide to J. K. Rowling and the Harry Potter Phenomenon*; *Fact, Fiction, and Folklore in Harry Potter's World: An Unofficial Guide*; and *Passport to Narnia: A Newcomer's Guide*. His website is www.georgebeahm.com.

Stan Goldin became an online merchant of Pokemon Cards and, later, Harry Potter merchandise after fleeing his executive life in the corporate world of finance and marketing. Based on his love of the first three Harry Potter books, and having heard rumors that the first book might be made into a movie, Goldin established the HP Wizard Store. At the time, there wasn't even any Harry Potter merchandise available to sell. After six years of peddling Harry Potter and related wizard products online, he opened his first brick and mortar store—Whimsic Alley. "My intention was not to create a store that simply sold Harry Potter branded merchandise. You can go to Wal-Mart for that. My goal was to build an environment where you might expect Harry and others in his wizarding community to shop themselves." Goldin hired Hollywood set designers to create such an environment, which includes the Phoenix Wands Shop, the Widdleshaft Quill Shop, Habber and Dasher's Robe and Apparel Shop, Pilcher & Bott's Confectioners, the Whimsic Owlery, Borgin & Crabbe's Curio Shop and, for those intent on purchasing Harry Potter branded merchandise, the original HP Wizard Store. His web site is www.whimsicalley.com.

Tim Kirk is a design director for Kirk Design, which draws on his vast experience in conceptualization, content creation, and art direction at Walt Disney Imagineering, where he worked for 22 years. Among his many credits at Disney, Kirk was the overall senior designer for Tokyo DisneySea, a three billion dollar theme park. He also played a key role in conceptualizing the popular Disney MGM Studio Tour Park in Walt Disney World. A five-time Hugo award winner for best art in the fantasy and science fiction field, Kirk has illustrated fanzines, calendars, limited edition books, and trade books for numerous publishers. Kirk Design's website is www.kirkdesigninc.com.

If You Liked This Book . . .

MUGGLES AND MAGIC:
AN UNOFFICIAL GUIDE TO
J. K. ROWLING AND THE
HARRY POTTER PHENOMENON

FACT, FICTION, AND
FOLKLORE IN HARRY
POTTER'S WORLD:
AN UNOFFICIAL GUIDE

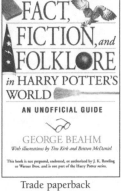

Trade paperback
382 pages • $17.95

Trade paperback
280 pages • $16.95

Both written by George Beahm, with illustrations by Tim Kirk.

If you liked *The Whimsic Alley Book of Spells,* you might want to try my earlier books on J. K. Rowling and Harry Potter: *Muggles and Magic* and *Fact, Fiction, and Folklore in Harry Potter's World.*

Muggles is a companion-style book that tells you everything you'd want to know about J. K. Rowling and Harry Potter: from the books to the movies, from interviews to revealing quotes, from fan trips overseas to coverage on the world of Harry Potter fandom—and full coverage of Rowling's NYC visit in 2006. The third edition has been extensively revised, updated, and expanded. Illustrated with photos and art, including a brand-new 16-page color section with photos of Harry Potter dolls from the Tonner Company and Rowling's NYC appearance, this book is indispensable reading for any Harry Potter fan.

Fact, Fiction, and Folklore is a look at the myths, historical references, and science found in Rowling's Harry Potter novels. Organized in four sections (fabulous beasts, prominent wizards, magical artifacts, and magical places), this book discusses in a fun and entertaining way the inspiration for the various critters, beasties, people, and places that populate the wizarding world.

Hampton Roads Publishing Company

... for the evolving human spirit

HAMPTON ROADS PUBLISHING COMPANY
publishes books on a variety of subjects,
including metaphysics, spirituality,
health, visionary fiction, and other related topics.

For a copy of our latest trade catalog,
call toll-free, 800-766-8009,
or send your name and address to:

HAMPTON ROADS PUBLISHING COMPANY, INC.
1125 STONEY RIDGE ROAD • CHARLOTTESVILLE, VA 22902
E-mail: hrpc@hrpub.com • Internet: www.hrpub.com